Level 2 • Book 2

Themes

Look Again

Courage

America's People

SRA Imagine It!

**Level 2
Book 2**

Program Authors

Carl Bereiter

Andy Biemiller

Joe Campione

Iva Carruthers

Doug Fuchs

Lynn Fuchs

Steve Graham

Karen Harris

Jan Hirshberg

Anne McKeough

Peter Pannell

Michael Pressley

Marsha Roit

Marlene Scardamalia

Marcy Stein

Gerald H. Treadway Jr.

McGraw Hill SRA

Columbus, OH

Acknowledgments

Grateful acknowledgement is given to the following publishers and copyright owners for permissions granted to reprint selections from their publications. All possible care has been taken to trace ownership and secure permission for each selection included. In case of any errors or omissions, the Publisher will be pleased to make suitable acknowledgements in future editions.

LOOK AGAIN

Animal Camouflage by Janet McDonnell, copyright 1998 © by The Child's World ®, Inc./www.childsworld.com. Reprinted by permission.

From HUNGRY LITTLE HARE, text copyright © 1998 by Howard Goldsmith, illustrations copyright © 1998 by Denny Bond. Reprinted with permission of Learning Triangle Press, an imprint of The McGraw-Hill Companies. All rights reserved.

HOW TO HIDE AN OCTOPUS AND OTHER SEA CREATURES by Ruth Heller. Copyright © by Ruth Heller, 1992. Published by arrangement with Grosset and Dunlap, a division of Penguin Young Readers Group, a division of Penguin Group (USA) Inc. All rights reserved.

HOW THE GUINEA FOWL GOT HER SPOTS by Barbara Knutson. Copyright 1990 by Barbara Knutson. Published by Carolrhoda Books, Inc. a division of the Lerner Publishing Group. Used by permission of the publisher. All rights reserved.

Text and adapted art from I SEE ANIMALS HIDING by Jim Arnosky. Copyright © 1995 by Jim Arnosky. All rights reserved. Used by permission of Scholastic Inc.

"Rabbit" Reprinted with the permission of Atheneum books for Young Readers, an imprint of Simon & Schuster Children's Publishing Division from FIREFLIES AT MIDNIGHT by Marilyn Singer. Text copyright © 2003 Marilyn Singer.

"The Tiger" from FUR, FANGS AND FOOTPRINTS by Patricia M. Stockland, illustrated by Sara Rojo Perez. Used with the permission of Picture Window Books.

COURAGE

"Dragons and Giants" from FROG AND TOAD TOGETHER COPYRIGHT © 1971, 1972 BY ARNOLD LOBEL. Used by permission of HarperCollins Publishers.

From THE HOLE IN THE DIKE by Norma Green, illustrated by Eric Carle. Text copyright © 1974 by Norma Green, illustration copyright © 1974 by Eric Carle. Reprinted by permission of Scholastic Inc.

Text and art from THE EMPTY POT by Demi. © 1990 by Demi. Reprinted by permission of Henry Holt and Company, LLC.

AKIAK by Robert J. Blake. Copyright © 1997 by Robert J. Blake. Published by arrangement with Philomel Books, a division of Penguin Young Readers Group, a division of Penguin Group (USA) Inc. All rights reserved.

BRAVE AS A MOUNTAIN LION by Ann Herbert Scott. Text copyright (c) 1996 by Ann Herbert Scott. Illustrations copyright © 1996 by Glo Coalson. Reprinted by permission of Clarion Books, an imprint of Houghton Mifflin Company. All rights reserved.

"Life Doesn't Frighten Me," copyright © 1978 by Maya Angelou, from AND STILL I RISE by Maya Angelou. Used by permission of Random House, Inc.

"Courage" from Hockey Cards & Hopscotch Study Book. With permission of Emily Hearn.

AMERICA'S PEOPLE

Reprinted with the permission of Simon & Schuster Books for Young Readers, an imprint of Simon & Schuster Children's Publishing Division from HOW MY FAMILY LIVES IN AMERICA by Susan Kuklin. Copyright © 1992 Susan Kuklin.

NEW HOPE by Henri Sorensen. COPYRIGHT © 1995 BY HENRI SORENSEN. Used by permission of HarperCollins Publishers.

A PICTURE BOOK OF MARTIN LUTHER KING, JR. Text copyright © 1989 by David A. Adler. Illustrations copyright © 1989 by Robert Casilla. All rights reserved. Reprinted by permission of Holiday House, Inc.

JINGLE DANCER by Cynthia Leitich Smith illustrated by Corneilus Van Wright and Ying-Hhwa Hu. COPYRIGHT © BY CYNTHIA LEITICH SMITH. Used by permission of HarperCollins Publishers.

CESAR E. CHAVEZ by Don McLeese. Rourke Publishing LLC, Vero Beach, FL 32964.

Reprinted with the permission of Margaret K. McElderry Books, an imprint of Simon & Schuster Children's Publishing Division from AMERICA IS . . . by Louise Borden, illustrated by Stacey Schuett. Text copyright © 2002 Louise Borden. Illustrations copyright © 2002 Stacey Schuett.

"Statue of Liberty" Reprinted with the permission of Margaret K. McElderry Books, an imprint of Simon & Schuster Children's Publishing Division from I NEVER TOLD AND OTHER POEMS by Myra Cohn Livingston. Copyright © 1992 Myra Cohn Livingston.

SRAonline.com

Send all inquiries to:
SRA/McGraw-Hill
4400 Easton Commons
Columbus, OH 43219

ISBN: 978-0-07-609644-2
MHID: 0-07-609644-0

1 2 3 4 5 6 7 8 9 RRW 14 13 12 11 10 09 08 07

The *McGraw·Hill* Companies

Program Authors

Carl Bereiter, Ph.D.
University of Toronto

Andy Biemiller, Ph.D.
University of Toronto

Joe Campione, Ph.D.
University of California, Berkeley

Iva Carruthers, Ph.D.
Northeastern Illinois University

Doug Fuchs, Ph.D.
Vanderbilt University

Lynn Fuchs, Ph.D.
Vanderbilt University

Steve Graham, Ed.D.
Vanderbilt University

Karen Harris, Ed.D.
Vanderbilt University

Jan Hirshberg, Ed.D.
Reading Specialist

Anne McKeough, Ph.D.
University of Toronto

Peter Pannell
Principal, Longfellow Elementary School,
Pasadena, California

Michael Pressley, Ph.D.
Michigan State University

Marsha Roit, Ed.D.
National Reading Consultant

Marlene Scardamalia, Ph.D.
University of Toronto

Marcy Stein, Ph.D.
University of Washington, Tacoma

Gerald H. Treadway, Jr., Ed.D.
San Diego State University

Look Again

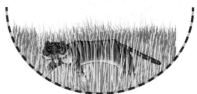

Unit 5 Table of Contents

Courage

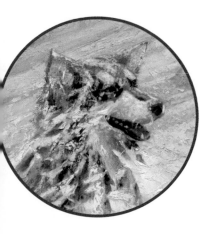

America's People

Look Again

Seeing is believing. Or is it? Can you always trust what you see? Can something look like one thing and really be something different? Maybe!

Theme Connection

Look at the photograph.

- What do you see?
- Is the lizard hard to see?
- How is the lizard hiding?

BIG Idea

Why do animals need to hide?

Animal Camouflage
by Janet McDonnell

Genre
Expository
Text is written to inform or explain. It contains facts about real people, things, or events.

Comprehension Skill
Main Idea and Details
As you read, identify the main idea of the selection and look for details to support the main idea.

Focus Questions
What is animal camouflage?
How is camouflage like wearing a costume?

Read the article to find the meanings of these words, which are also in "Animal Camouflage":

✦ camouflage
✦ mimicry
✦ patterns
✦ surroundings
✦ pretenders
✦ blend

Vocabulary Strategy

Use **context clues** to find the meanings of *blend* and *mimicry*.

Vocabulary

Warm-Up

Will and Dion were walking through the woods.

"Do you think there are animals here?" Dion asked Will.

"I have not seen any," Will said.

Many animals were using camouflage, or a disguise, to hide from them.

A green lizard was using mimicry. Its skin had patterns. It looked like the leaves on a tree.

"I think there are animals here who match their surroundings," Dion said.

"What do you mean?" Will asked.

"Some animals are pretenders," Dion explained. "This makes them hard to see."

"So animals can blend in?" Will asked.

"Yes," said Dion. "Do you see that tree?"

Will looked up at the tree. A bird flew from it. He had not seen the bird until now.

"I think there *are* animals hiding here," Will said.

Guessing Game
Choose a partner. Ask your partner, "What word means 'to mix together'?" After correctly guessing *blend*, it is your partner's turn to choose a word for you to guess. Review all the vocabulary words.

Concept Vocabulary

The concept word for this lesson is **protection.** *Protection* is "the keeping of someone or something from harm." Many animals use colors and patterns for protection. How does an animal's color provide protection for it?

Genre

Expository **Text** is written to inform or explain. It contains facts about real people, things, or events.

Comprehension Skill

Main Idea and Details

As you read, identify the main idea of the selection and look for details to support the main idea.

Animal

by Janet McDonnell

Camouflage

Focus Questions

What is animal camouflage?
How is camouflage like wearing
a costume?

What Is Camouflage?

Have you ever played hide and seek outside? Sometimes it is hard to find a good place to hide! But what if you could paint yourself brown and green like the ground?

Or put on a costume that made you look like a tree? Or lie down and cover yourself with leaves? All of these tricks would make you much harder to find.

A forest looks green and brown.

What Is Camouflage?

Some animals use tricks to hide themselves. Using colors and patterns to hide is called camouflage. Camouflage makes things very hard to find—even when they are out in the open.

A walkingstick looks like the branches around it.

Animals, fish, reptiles, and even people use camouflage for hiding. When something looks like the objects around it, it is much harder to see. That is what camouflage is all about!

Why Do Animals Need Camouflage?

There are many reasons why animals hide. They often hide from their enemies. Some animals move around at night and sleep during the day. They need to stay hidden while they sleep.

This emperor moth has an eyespot on its wing to scare enemies.

Other animals hide so that they can be better hunters. Camouflage helps them sneak up on their dinner.

How Do Animals Use Camouflage?

Animals use camouflage in many different ways. Some use it to blend in with the objects around them. These objects are called surroundings. The *polar bear's* white coat blends in with its surroundings—the white snow. This color hides the bear when it is hunting for seals.

The white fur of this polar bear looks like the snow around it.

The *black bear's* dark coat helps it hide in dark trees and bushes.

But what happens if an animal's surroundings are more than one color? Some animals have camouflage with more than one color, too!

Some fish have dark backs and white bellies. When a hungry bird looks into the dark water, the fish's dark back is hard to see. But to an enemy deeper in the water, the fish's white belly blends in with the bright sky.

This large mouth bass has a dark back that matches the water.

Why Do Some Animals Change Color?

Sometimes an animal's surroundings change. Then the animal has to change color, too! That is the only way it can stay hidden. Some animals change color to match the season. The *snowshoe rabbit* changes color very slowly in the spring and fall.

In the winter, the snowshoe rabbit's fur is white like the snow. As the snow melts in the spring, the rabbit grows patches of brown fur. It looks just like patches of ground and melting snow.

This snowshoe rabbit has white fur to match the snow.

This baby snowshoe rabbit has brown fur in the spring.

Then summer comes, and the ground is brown. The rabbit's fur grows brown to match. When fall comes, the rabbit starts to turn white again.

Do All Animals Use Colors to Hide?

Some animals use designs, or patterns, instead of changing colors. Blending into a pattern is a good way to hide. When an animal's body looks like its surroundings, it is very hard to find.

Fawns like this one can blend into their surroundings.

A fawn, or baby deer, is too weak to run fast. But it can hide by lying still. The fawn's back is covered with dots. The dots look like spots of sunlight on the forest floor. If the fawn stays still, it is very hard to see.

This bittern has patterns that match the tall grass.

Another animal that uses patterns to hide is the *bittern.* This bird lives in marshes with tall grass. The stripes on its feathers look just like shadows in the grass.

When the bittern is in danger, it makes itself even harder to find. It points its beak straight up and sways its body in the breeze. The bittern looks just like the blowing grass!

What Is Mimicry?

Some animals have a shape or color that looks like something else. This type of camouflage is called mimicry. Animals that use mimicry are good pretenders.

The *walkingstick* is one insect that uses mimicry. Its long, thin, bumpy body looks just like a small branch!

This walkingstick looks like a branch.

Walkingsticks can even change color with the seasons. In the spring, the tree's branches and leaves are green. The walkingstick is green, too. When the branches and leaves turn brown, the walkingstick turns brown to match.

Some animals use other kinds of mimicry to fool their enemies. Some moths have large spots on their rear wings. The spots look just like eyes!

When the moth is resting, its front wings cover the spots. But when the moth senses danger, it lifts its front wings and shows the spots. If an enemy is afraid of the big "eyes," it will leave the moth alone.

Some animals even make their own costumes for camouflage. The *masked crab* uses seaweed to make a costume.

This masked crab has used many things to make its costume.

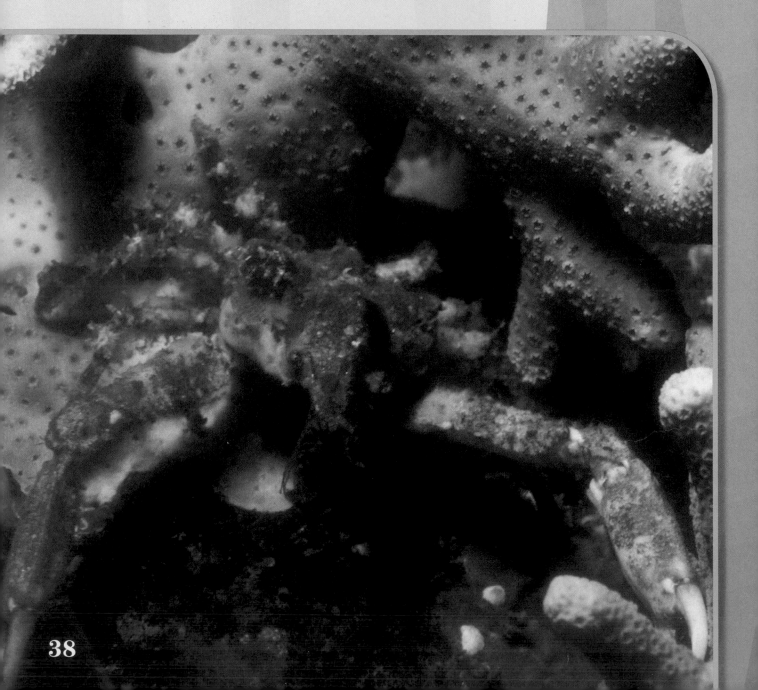

First the crab uses its claws to tear the seaweed into pieces. Then it puts each piece in its mouth and chews it until it is soft. The crab sticks the pieces of seaweed to itself. Little hooks on its shell and legs hold the seaweed in place.

This zale moth is hard to see because it looks like the tree trunk.

From a rabbit that changes color to a crab in a seaweed costume, there are many kinds of camouflage. But each kind of camouflage has the same important job—to help animals hide.

Now that you know some of their tricks, maybe you will see animals where you never saw them before. But you'll have to look very carefully, or you might be fooled!

Janet McDonnell

McDonnell came up with the idea for writing "Animal Camouflage" during a brainstorming session with publishers. Because she loves animals, she was excited to be given the chance to write about them. When she writes about a subject, she likes to research it very carefully. Sometimes she gets so much information that she cannot use it because the book can only be so long. Then her challenge is to get the ideas across in a clear and interesting way. "My goal is to make the reader as excited about the topic as I am," she said.

Theme Connections

Within the Selection

1. What are some of the different ways animals use camouflage?

2. Why do some animals have so much color or have special markings?

3. Which animals were the most difficult to find in the photographs?

Beyond the Selection

4. Where have you noticed animals using camouflage?

5. Did you have to look carefully to find them?

Write about It!

Describe an animal that uses colors or special markings to hide.

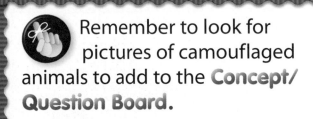

Remember to look for pictures of camouflaged animals to add to the **Concept/ Question Board.**

Science Inquiry

Genre

Newspaper Articles tell about people, places, or things that happen in nations, states, and cities.

Feature

Quotations are statements made by people in an article or a story.

THE NORTHERN GAZETTE

Smart Bears
Sleep the Winter Away

by Maria Gonzo

Scientist Jill Barker knows all about bears. She has studied them in their natural surroundings for ten years.

"Bear cubs are born in January or February," she says. "They stay in their mother's care for seventeen months."

Barker says brown bears are smart. "They have large brains and good memories. They also prepare for winter." Bears eat a lot of food before winter. This helps keep their bodies warm. Then they hibernate, or sleep, for as long as seven months.

"Like I said, bears are smart. They eat a lot of food before it gets cold. Then they sleep through the winter!"

1. How do you know Jill Barker thinks bears are smart?

2. Why might a bear cub stay with its mother for seventeen months?

3. Explain how bears prepare for winter.

Try It!

As you work on your investigation, remember to look in newspaper articles for facts and information.

Read the article to find the meanings of these words, which are also in "Hungry Little Hare":

✦ meadow
✦ pond
✦ scent
✦ disguise
✦ hare
✦ stump

Vocabulary Strategy

Use **apposition** to find the meanings of *scent* and *hare*.

Vocabulary

Warm-Up

Spring had barely begun. A red-winged blackbird flew high above the meadow. Turtles were basking in the morning sun. They were happy to be out of the deep mud from the bottom of the pond where they spent the winter.

The scent, or smell, of violets told the animals that the cold was over. "Time to make my nest," said the blackbird. The blackbird knew she must disguise her nest in the tall grass.

She made her nest in the shape of an open cup. It was woven between stems of spring grass. The grass was still soggy from the spring rains.

A hare, a kind of rabbit, hopped through the new grass. She sat near a stump waiting for her young to catch up to her.

The warm sun was high in the sky. All the animals felt a little drowsy. The turtles napped. The rabbits slept cuddled up to their mother.

Only the blackbird did not nap. She was busy laying her eggs.

GAME

Fill In the Blank

On a sheet of paper, use each of the vocabulary words in a sentence. Draw a blank line in place of the vocabulary word. Give your paper to another student. Have your partner fill in each blank with the correct vocabulary word.

Concept Vocabulary

The concept word for this lesson is **environment.** The *environment* is the things that surround a person, an animal, or a plant, such as the air, the water, and the weather. How might an animal's environment change during the year?

Hungry Little Hare

by Howard Goldsmith

illustrated by Denny Bond

Focus Questions

Can animals ever be in danger because they are camouflaged? Have you ever accidentally stepped on an animal or a creature?

Little Hare the jackrabbit had great long ears with little black tips. Her long furry hind paws helped her hop very fast and jump very high.

One beautiful day, Little Hare smelled raspberries. Raspberry leaves were her favorite food.

Little Hare hopped, and then she hopped
again. She followed the scent of raspberry to
a pond in the meadow.

"Ouch!" a voice cried. "You stepped on
me!" Little Hare looked, but she saw only
bright green grass.

"I can't see you," Little Hare said.

"You're not supposed to see me," said a green frog, hopping in front of Little Hare. "My color hides me in the grass from snoopy snakes. *You* don't eat frogs, do you?"

"Oh, no!" said Little Hare. "I'm looking for raspberry leaves."

Little Hare hopped, and then she hopped again. *Crunch, crunch, crunch* went the twigs in the woods.

"Ouch!" a voice cried. "You pushed me!"

Little Hare looked, but she saw only brown twigs on a tree stump.

"I can't see you," Little Hare said.

"You're not supposed to see me," said a walkingstick, crawling up to Little Hare. "I look exactly like a twig. That's how I hide from sneaky squirrels."

Little Hare was hungry. She hopped, and then she hopped again, past a big green bush.

"Ouch!" a voice said. "You bumped me!"

Little Hare looked, but she saw only slender green leaves.

"I can't see you," Little Hare said.

"You're not supposed to see me!" A katydid hopped up right in front of Little Hare. "I look exactly like a leaf, but I'm really an insect. My disguise protects me from prying praying mantises."

Now Little Hare was *very* hungry. She hopped, and then hopped again, and leaned against a tree to rest.

"Ouch!" said a voice. "Don't lean on me!"

Little Hare looked and looked, but she saw only brown bark on the tree.

"I can't see you," said Little Hare. "I guess you look like something else, too."

"That's right," said a moth, fluttering in front of Little Hare. "My color matches the bark of a tree, so when I rest the wily woodpeckers can't find me."

Little Hare was just about to hop off when a drowsy voice exclaimed, "Careful! I'm resting in the leaves at your feet!"

Little Hare looked down just as a woodcock shook out his feathers.

"I blend into the leaves on the ground to avoid furry foxes," he explained.

Little Hare was so hungry she could barely hop. But she spied some lovely lilies nearby.

She was just about to sniff them when a voice cried, "Don't sneeze!"

Little Hare looked, but she saw only yellow lilies.

"I can't see you," Little Hare said.

"You're not supposed to see me," replied a crab spider. "Leaping lizards think I'm a flower, but I only look like one. I can change color to match many kinds of flowers, so I'm invisible wherever I go."

"Well, I'm just a jackrabbit," said Little
Hare, "and I'm going to find my mother."

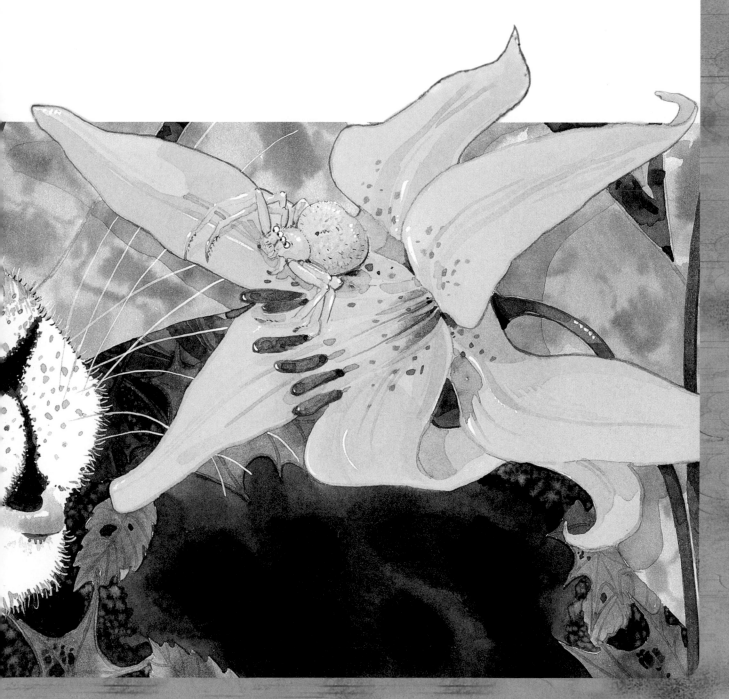

Soon Little Hare found her mother among tender, juicy raspberry leaves!

"Mother, what does *invisible* mean?" asked Little Hare as she munched.

"It means you disappear into the world around you," explained her mother.

"I wish I were invisible like the other animals and insects," said Little Hare.

"You will be," replied her mother. "You only have to wait."

And Mother Hare was right!

Meet the Author

Howard Goldsmith

Goldsmith writes articles for magazines and encyclopedias, but he thinks there is something special about writing children's books. It is fun for him to use his imagination to come up with ideas that children will like to read about.

Meet the Illustrator

Denny Bond

In addition to children's books, Bond has done illustrations for magazines and advertisements. He is also a painter. He tells young artists, "Dream with your eyes open . . . and always carry paper and pencil for doodling, or at least to write down ideas that may pop into your head . . . ."

Look Again

Theme Connections

Within the Selection

1. Why was Little Hare unable to see the other animals and insects?

2. How did Little Hare become invisible?

Across Selections

3. Which animals that you read about in this story were also in "Animal Camouflage"?

Beyond the Selection

4. Have you ever not seen something because it was hidden? What was it?

5. Think about how "Hungry Little Hare" adds to what you know about camouflage.

Write about It!

Describe a time you saw a rabbit. Was it hiding?

Remember to look for pictures of camouflaged animals to add to the **Concept/Question Board.**

Science Inquiry

Food Chains and Food Webs

Some animals eat plants, and some animals eat other animals. A **food chain** shows how each living thing gets its food. For example, a simple food chain links grass to grasshoppers to frogs to hawks. All these animals live in or visit the same area, such as a pond or a meadow. The diagram of the food chain shows that grasshoppers eat grass, frogs eat grasshoppers, and hawks eat frogs.

Most animals are part of more than one food chain and eat more than one kind of food in order to meet their food and energy requirements. These interconnected food chains form a **food web.** A food web shows how plants and animals are connected in many ways to help them all survive.

Think Link

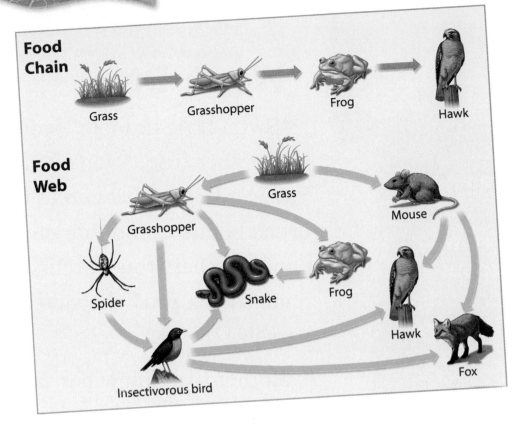

Food Chain

Grass → Grasshopper → Frog → Hawk

Food Web

Grasshopper
Grass
Mouse
Spider
Snake
Frog
Hawk
Fox
Insectivorous bird

1. How are the diagrams of the food chain and the food web helpful?

2. According to the food web, what animals do snakes eat?

3. Look at the diagram of the food web, and explain how all the animals depend on grass to survive.

Try It!

As you work on your investigation, think about how you can use a diagram to show your facts.

Read the article to find the meanings of these words, which are also in "How to Hide an Octopus and Other Sea Creatures":

✦ delay
✦ glides
✦ designed
✦ proceeds
✦ fade
✦ creatures

Vocabulary Strategy

Use **context clues** to find the meanings of *designed, fade,* and *creatures.*

Vocabulary

Warm-Up

"Swim little tadpole," said the mother frog. "Don't delay!" Tadpole began to swim to the green plants at the side of the pond. Mother frog watched. "He glides like a pro," she said to herself.

Mother frog knew her tadpole was designed to swim. His whole body looked like a little tail. "Swim faster!" she called. "He proceeds just like he should," she thought.

The plants were baking in the hot sun. Their color had started to

fade. "Hurry little tadpole," said Mother frog. "The plants will fail to hide you if they fade anymore."

Other creatures watched little tadpole. A toad sat close by. She croaked a loud "hello" to Mother frog.

"Swim little tadpole," said Mother frog. Tadpole swam faster. "Home at last!" said Mother frog.

Tadpole felt very tired. "That's because you are changing every day," said Mother frog. "Soon you will be a frog just like me."

Days passed. The little tadpole turned into a frog. He did not glide anymore. Now he hopped from lily pad to lily pad!

GAME

Memory Game
Write each vocabulary word on an index card. Then write each word's meaning on its own card. Turn over and spread out the cards. Take turns with a partner, matching each word with its meaning.

Concept Vocabulary

The concept word for this lesson is **survive.** *Survive* means "to stay alive." Animals stay alive by living in safe places. Where would a frog live to survive?

Genre

Rhyming Nonfiction tells people something. It uses rhyme to present facts and information in an entertaining way.

Comprehension Strategy

⭐ **Clarifying**
As you read, check to make sure you understand what you are reading and clarify any difficult words or phrases.

How to Hide an Octopus

& other sea creatures

by Ruth Heller

Focus Questions

Are land animals the only creatures that use camouflage? If you were a sea creature, how would you hide from your enemies?

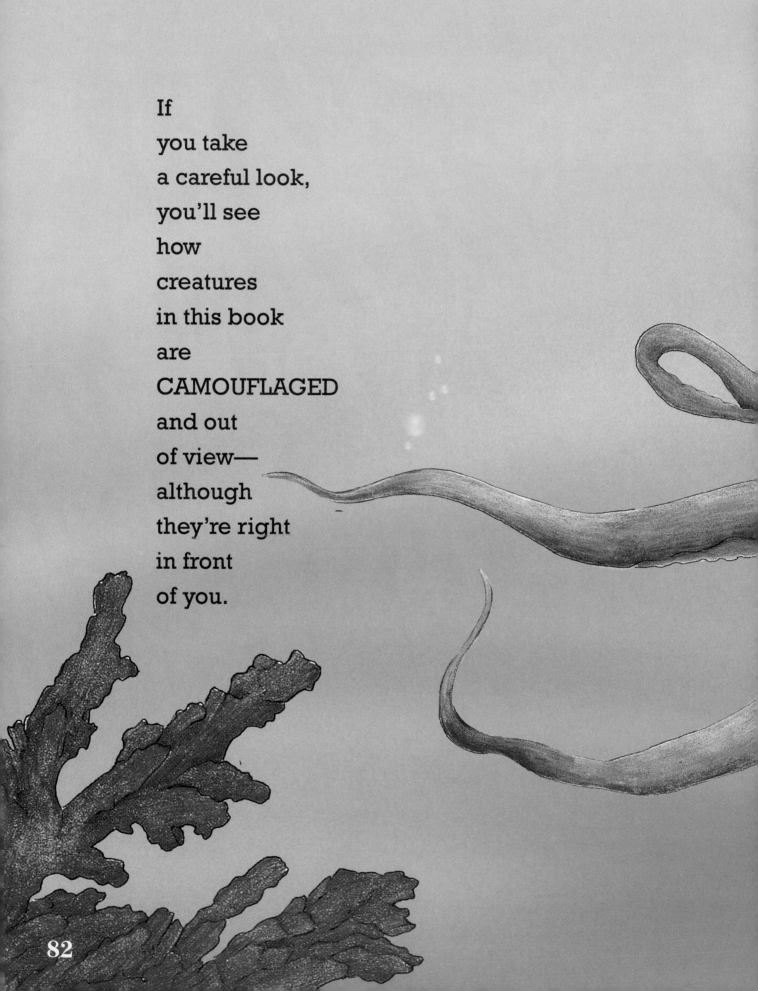

If
you take
a careful look,
you'll see
how
creatures
in this book
are
CAMOUFLAGED
and out
of view—
although
they're right
in front
of you.

As quick as a wink,
it turns to pink
or green or blue
or any hue,
and, if you think
that's not enough,
its skin can
turn
from
smooth to
rough.

This
creature
is an
OCTOPUS
and very often
hides

by
changing
to the
color . . .

over
which
it glides.

85

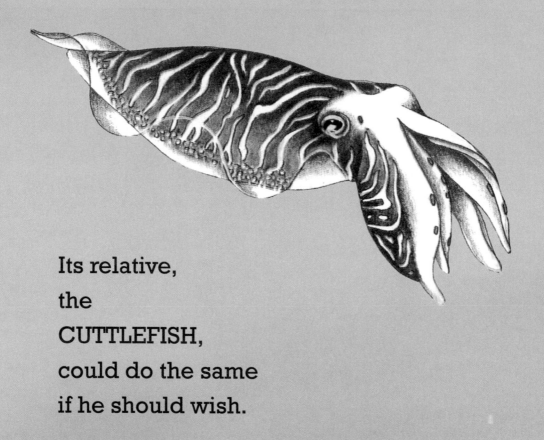

Its relative,
the
CUTTLEFISH,
could do the same
if he should wish.

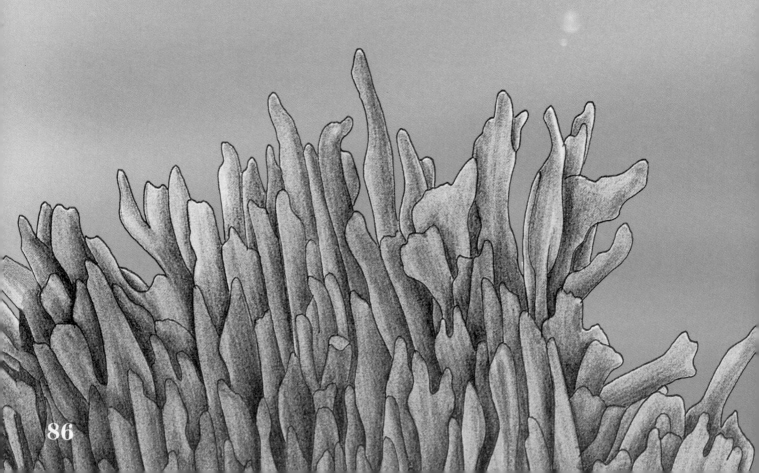

The stripes that he is
sporting
show
that he's
been courting,
but
he can
make them
fade away . . .

slowly
or
without
delay.

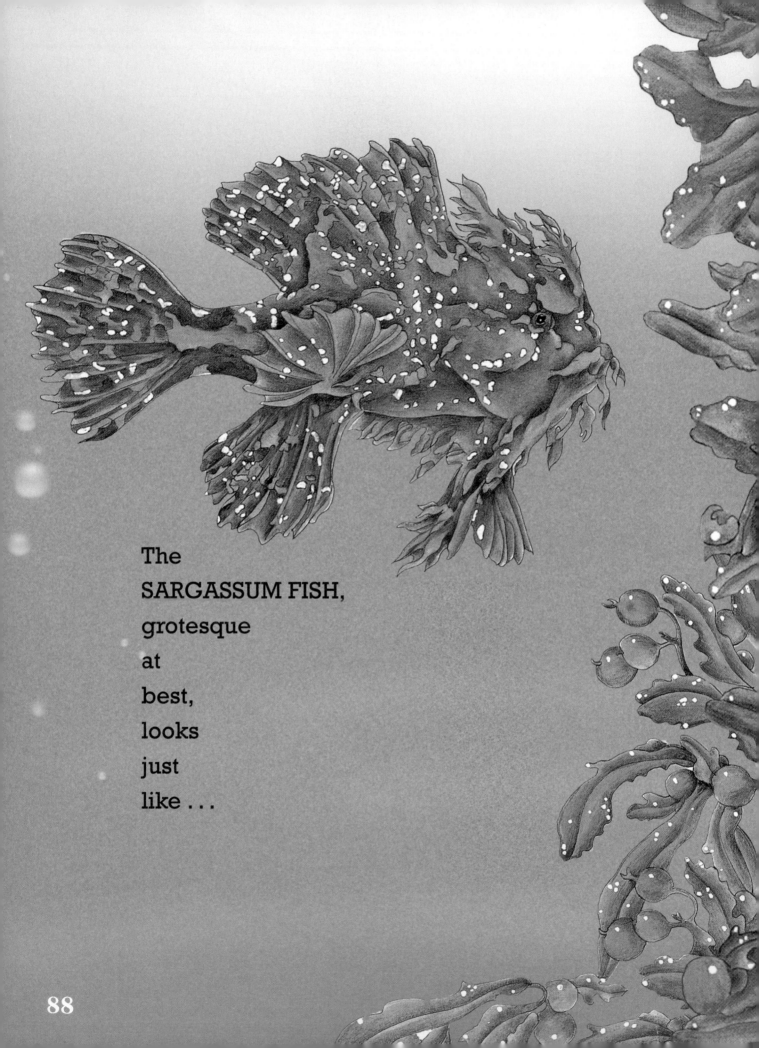

The
SARGASSUM FISH,
grotesque
at
best,
looks
just
like . . .

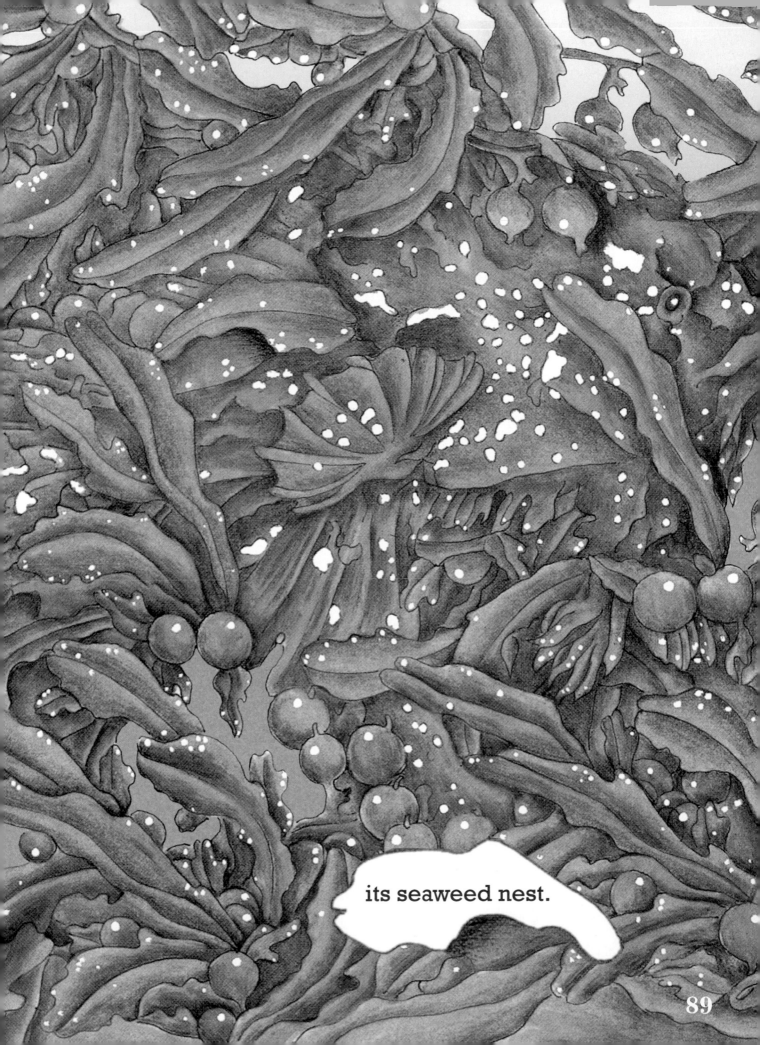

its seaweed nest.

The
giant red
SEA DRAGON
is
the most bizarre
of all the
creatures
seen so far,
with
ribbons of skin
that grow
from its chin
and
from its
belly and back.

They
spread
from its head
and trail from its tail,
and it's
easy to see
why its enemies fail
to find
where it feeds . . .
among the red weeds.

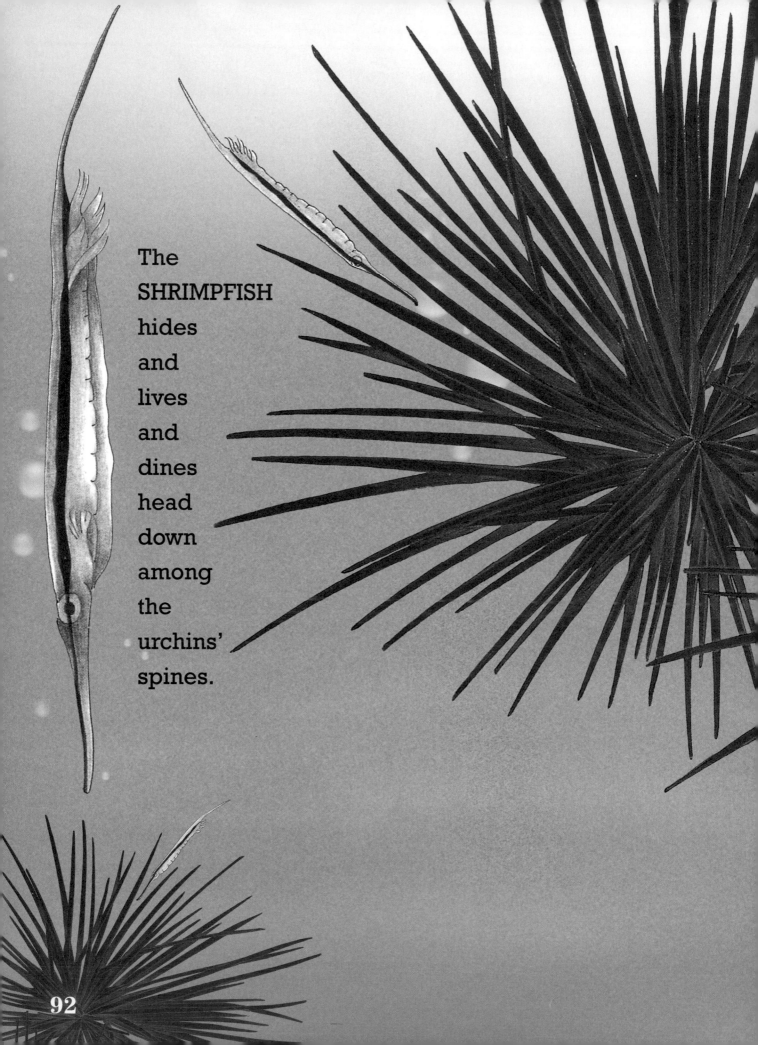

The
SHRIMPFISH
hides
and
lives
and
dines
head
down
among
the
urchins'
spines.

92

Heads
up,
the
PIPEFISH
like
to
play
and
with
the
grasses
drift
and
sway.

The
BUTTERFLY
FISH
has been
designed

to
make
it
very
hard . . .
to
find.

The
DECORATOR CRAB
is drab
and
will not rest
until it's dressed,

96

so
it proceeds
to don
some
weeds
and barnacles
and sponge,
you
see,

and
even
an . . .
anemone.

97

Meet the Author and Illustrator

Ruth Heller

Heller began her career designing wrapping paper, napkins, kites, mugs, and greeting cards. She even designed coloring books. Once when she was studying tropical fish for a coloring book she was making, Heller saw a strange-looking shape floating in the fish tank. It was an egg sac. Heller began to read about egg-laying animals. She thought about the eggs in the fish tank. Colorful shapes and words began to go through her mind. That was when she decided to write and illustrate children's books. Her first book was called *Chickens Aren't the Only Ones*.

Look Again

Theme Connections

Within the Selection

1. How does an octopus hide?

2. Why do sea creatures need camouflage?

Across Selections

3. How is "How to Hide an Octopus and Other Sea Creatures" like the other stories you have read? How is it different?

Beyond the Selection

4. What other sea creatures can you name?

Write about It!

Describe a time you saw an animal hiding.

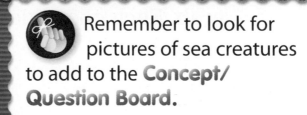

Remember to look for pictures of sea creatures to add to the **Concept/Question Board.**

Science Inquiry

Creatures in Costume

Have you ever played hide-and-seek? Sometimes it is hard to find a good place to hide! But what if you could put on a costume that made you look like a tree?

Some animals make their own costumes for camouflage. The masked crab uses seaweed to make a costume.

First the crab tears the seaweed into pieces. Then it chews each piece and sticks the pieces of seaweed to itself. Little hooks on its shell and legs hold the seaweed in place.

The masked crab uses its costume to hide on the Atlantic Ocean's floor. Other sea creatures cannot see the crab. Each one glides by the hidden crab.

1. How does the masked crab use seaweed to survive?

2. How is the map helpful?

3. Choose a sea creature you want to learn more about. Use sources, such as the Internet and an encyclopedia, to find out where it lives. Write your creature's name on a sticky note, and place it on a map to show others where it lives.

Try It!

As you work on your investigation, think about how you can use a map to show your facts.

Read the article to find the meanings of these words, which are also in "How the Guinea Fowl Got Her Spots":

✦ **delicate**
✦ **reeds**
✦ **bank**
✦ **admired**
✦ **temper**
✦ **glossy**

Vocabulary Strategy

Use **apposition** to find the meanings of *temper* and *glossy*.

Vocabulary

Warm-Up

The delicate little cow looked surprised as Leo patted her. Leo looked gratefully at his grandma. He had wanted a cow forever. Now he had one that was just perfect.

"Where will she go when it is very hot?" Leo asked his grandma.

"We have reeds and trees near the bank of the pond. Her little body will be cool there," answered Leo's grandma. "She will be admired by many people."

"Why?" asked Leo.

"Because she will give milk to many people," said Leo's grandma.

"What should I name her?" asked Leo.

"Let me think," answered his grandma. "She seems sweet and does not have a mean temper, or mood. Maybe you could name her Happy."

Leo thought for a minute. Then he looked at his new little cow. The sun made her coat look glossy and bright. "I think I will call her Sunshine," he said. "Sunshine is a perfect name!"

Flash Cards
Make a set of flash cards with the vocabulary words. Write the word on one side and its definition on the other side. Use the flash cards to review the vocabulary words and definitions. Then ask a partner to use the cards to quiz you.

Concept Vocabulary

The concept word for this lesson is **adapt.** *Adapt* means "to change in order to fit a specific use or situation." Leo's cow will adapt to the hot weather by spending more time in the shade by the pond. Why is it necessary for animals to adapt to their environments?

How the Guinea Fowl Got Her Spots

retold and illustrated
by Barbara Knutson

Focus Questions

Do you think animals look out for each other? In what ways? Do animals have a warning system to alert other animals of danger?

A long time ago, when everything had just been made, Nganga the Guinea Fowl had glossy black feathers all over. She had no white speckles as she does today—not a single spot.

Guinea Fowl was a little bird, but she had a big friend. And that was Cow.

They liked to go to the great green hills where Cow could eat grass and Nganga could scratch for seeds and crunch grasshoppers.

And they would both keep an eye out for Lion.

One day, Guinea Fowl was crossing the river to meet Cow on the most delicious hill they knew. The grass was so juicy and thick that, even from the river, Nganga could hear Cow hungrily tearing up one mouthful after another.

But . . . what was that Nganga saw slinking toward Cow?

Was it . . . ?

Yes, it was LION!

Now you might think a guinea fowl is no match for a lion, but Nganga didn't think that. In fact, she didn't think at all.

She scratched and scrambled up the bank as fast as she could and whirred right between Cow and Lion, kicking and flapping in the dust.

"RAAUGH!" shouted Lion.

"My eyes! This sand! What was that?"

When the clouds of dust thinned there was no sign of anyone—certainly not any dinner for Lion. He went home in a terrible temper, growling like his empty belly.

The next day, Guinea Fowl was at the grassy patch first. You can be sure she had her eyes wide open for Lion.

Soon she saw Cow cautiously crossing the river to join her—shlip, clop, shlop. But something yellow was twitching in the reeds.

Wasn't that Lion's tail?

Up whirred Nganga, half tumbling, half flying with her stubby wings. Lion looked up, startled, from his hiding place. Frrrr . . . a little black whirlwind was racing across the grass toward the river. "Whe-klo-klo-klo!" it called out to Cow.

"Guinea Fowl! That's where the duststorm came from yesterday," growled Lion between his sharp teeth. But the next moment, the whirlwind hit the river.

"RAAUghmf!" Lion exploded with a roar that ended underwater.

"I'll teach that bird to chase away my dinner!" he spluttered. But by the time his roar was working properly again, Cow and Guinea Fowl were safely over the next hill at Cow's house.

"Nganga," mooed Cow gratefully, "twice you have helped me escape from Lion. Now I will help you do the same."

Turning around, she dipped her tasseled tail into a calabash of milk. Then she shook the tasselful of milk over Guinea Fowl's sleek black feathers—flick, flock, flick—spattering her with creamy white milk.

Guinea Fowl craned her head and admired the delicate speckles covering her back.

She spread her wings, and Cow sprinkled them with milk too—flick, flock, flick.

"Whe-klo-klo! That's beautiful, Cow!" chuckled Nganga. "Thank you, my friend!"

And she set off for home.

Whom should she meet where the path crossed the river but Lion, still shaking the water out of his ears and angrier than ever.

"Ho, Speckled Bird!" snorted Lion. "Have you seen Guinea Fowl on your path?"

"Oh yes," clucked Nganga, hiding a smile. "I believe she went that way."

She pointed with her spotted wing to the hills far down the river.

"If you go quickly and don't stop to rest, you may catch up with her in a few days."

Lion leaped up at once, not bothering to thank the strange bird. A minute later, he thought about taking her along for a traveling snack, but when he looked back at the riverbank, he could see no trace of her.

"These lovely spots are just the thing for hiding in the shadows and grass!" laughed Nganga, who was, in fact, right where Lion had left her.

And she turned back to Cow's house to thank her friend again.

Barbara Knutson

Knutson was born in South Africa. She studied art in Africa and the United States. After receiving a degree in art education and French, she taught English and French in an international school in Nigeria.

Having grown up in South Africa and having traveled to other African countries, Knutson had a lot of personal experiences to use in her illustrations. Her detailed watercolors show the love and knowledge she had of African culture.

Look Again

Theme Connections

Within the Selection

1. How did Guinea Fowl protect her friend Cow from Lion?

2. How did Cow help protect Guinea Fowl?

Across Selections

3. How is Guinea Fowl's camouflage like the camouflage of other animals you have read about in this unit? How is it different?

Beyond the Selection

4. Think about how "How the Guinea Fowl Got Her Spots" adds to what you know about camouflage.

Write about It!

Describe a bird you have seen in your backyard. Did it have spots? How did it hide?

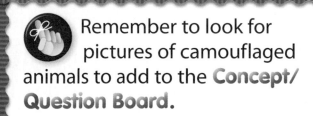

Remember to look for pictures of camouflaged animals to add to the **Concept/ Question Board.**

OUR FARM

Genre

Narrative Text is written from a first-person point of view. It is an account of personal events.

Feature

Words such as *I, my,* and *our* let you know this story is a narrative.

I live on a dairy farm. My family's farm has more than one hundred cows.

Each cow on our farm eats about forty pounds of hay and about fifty pounds of a special seed mixture each day. That is more than a person eats in one week!

Each cow on our farm drinks a lot of water too. I try to drink six glasses of water each day. But cows on our farm drink a bathtub full of water each day!

All this food and water make the cows produce more milk. The cows get milked three times every day. Then the milk is stored in a large cooler until a truck comes to get it. Finally the milk ends up in a grocery store.

Selling milk is how my family makes money. I have always admired my dad's job on our dairy farm. I would like to be in charge of it some day.

1. How does the narrator's family make money?

2. What words help you know the story is a narrative?

3. Why do you think a cow drinks so much more water than a person?

Try It!

As you work on your investigation, present some of your facts in the form of a narrative story to make the information more interesting.

Read the article to find the meanings of these words, which are also in "I See Animals Hiding":

- ✦ unaware
- ✦ protective
- ✦ coloration
- ✦ imitator
- ✦ available
- ✦ natural

Vocabulary Strategy

The prefix *un-* means "not." Use **word structure** to determine the meaning of *unaware.*

Vocabulary

Warm-Up

The tiny frog was unaware he was being watched. The fox stayed hidden in the thick brush by the stream. He watched the frog.

"That protective lily pad is the same color as the frog. I can barely see him!" said the fox.

The tiny frog sat quietly. He felt safe. The frog knew the coloration of his skin looked the same as the plants around him.

The cool spring air began to make the fox shiver. "I am cold," he said.

"I am also very hungry. I hope that frog moves soon!"

Time passed. The fox thought and thought. Finally he began wading into the water.

"I can be an imitator. Perhaps the frog will think I am a floating log," thought the clever fox. The fox was wrong.

The frog hopped away to another available lily pad in deeper water. He was even more clever than the fox. "It is natural for me to stay away from you," said the frog to the fox. "You will have a hard time catching me!"

GAME

Sentence Building

Work with a partner to create sentences using the vocabulary words. Choose a word from the list, and challenge your partner to make up a sentence using the word. Then switch roles. Continue until all the vocabulary words have been used.

Concept Vocabulary

The concept word for this lesson is **invisible.** *Invisible* means "not able to be seen." The frog was hard to see because the frog's color matched the lily pad. What other animals use colors and patterns to make themselves invisible?

Expository Text is written to inform or explain. It contains facts about real people, things, or events.

Comprehension Strategy

⭐ **Summarizing** As you read, use your own words to sum up the important points and information in the story.

Focus Questions

What are some different ways animals hide from their enemies? How can you see animals hiding?

I See Animals Hiding

by Jim Arnosky

I see animals hiding. I see a porcupine high in a tree.

Wild animals are shy and always hiding. It is natural for them to be this way. There are many dangers in the wild.

Even when they are caught unaware out in the open, wild animals try to hide. They stay behind whatever is available—a thin tree trunk or even a single blade of grass. Most of the time they go unnoticed.

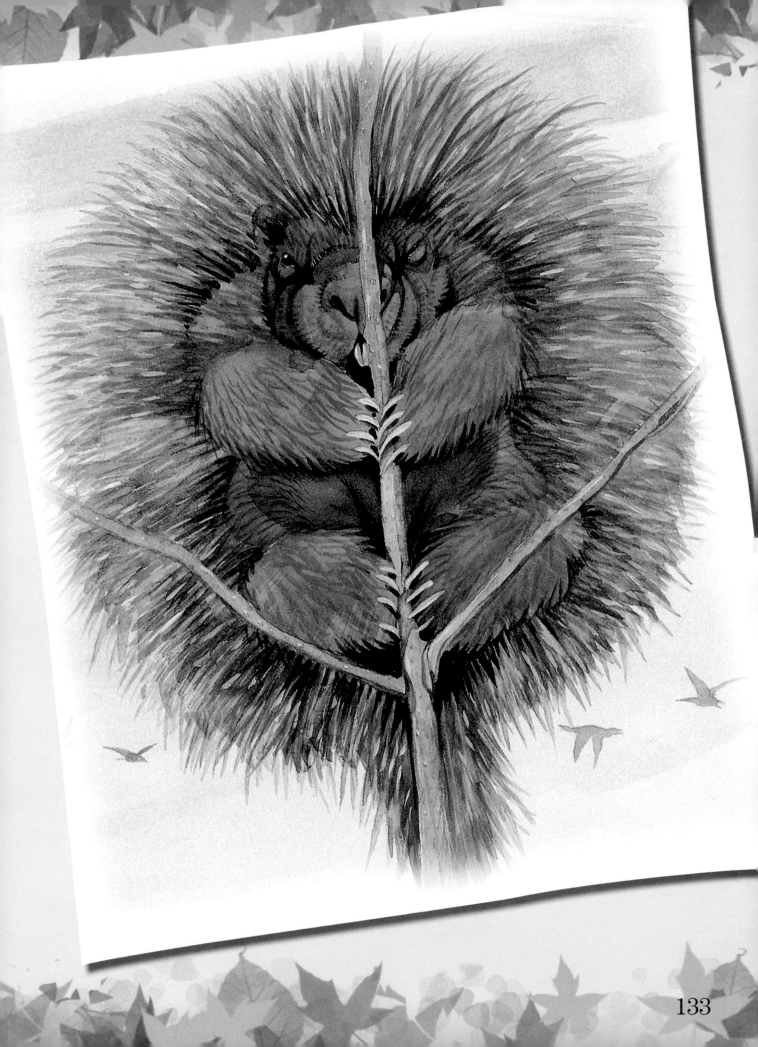

The colors of wild animals match the colors of the places where the animals live. Because of this protective coloration, called camouflage, wild animals can hide by simply staying still and blending in.

Woodcocks and other birds, which spend much of their time on the woodland floor, have patterns and colors like those of dry leaves.

I see animals hiding. I see two woodcocks on the leafy ground.

Of all wild animals, deer are the wariest. Even though their colors are camouflaged, they feel safe only where there are good hiding places nearby.

In a summer meadow of tall grasses and small shrubby trees, deer can hide quickly by just lying down.

In autumn, deer shed their red-brown summer coats and replace them with warmer, grayer winter coats that better match the gray and brown trunks of leafless trees.

I see animals hiding. I see a whole herd of deer on a winter hill.

There are 20 deer on the snow hill. Can you find them all?

Snowshoe hares change from summer brown to winter white. The only way to spot a snowshoe hare in a snowy scene is to look for its shiny black eyes.

Squint your eyes and you will see just how invisible a snowshoe hare on snow can be.

Here are three more animals that are as white as snow. The arctic fox and long-tailed weasel change from winter white to summer brown. The snowy owl stays white year-round.

Besides an owl, there is one other bark imitator on this tree. Can you tell what it is?

The colors and patterns of screech owls blend perfectly with tree bark. These small owls can sleep all day out in the open and not be discovered.

I see animals hiding. I see an owl and a moth on a limb.

Trout are camouflaged by color and shape to blend with the smooth mossy stones in a stream.

Looking down in a brook, I see a speckled trout swimming amid speckled stones.

I see animals hiding. I see a garter snake slithering through the grass.

Up close a snake in the grass may be easy to see. But as long as the snake keeps a safe distance from its enemies, it can sneak by, looking like just another broken branch on the ground.

Stand back a few steps from this page, and using only your eyes, try to follow the line of the snake from its head to its tail. Can you tell what is snake and what is stick?

A bittern is a wading bird whose brown streaks and long sticklike legs naturally blend in with the cattails and reeds that grow along shorelines.

When a bittern really needs to be invisible, it points its bill upward and sways its long neck, like a cattail swaying gently in a breeze.

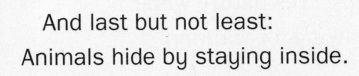

And last but not least:
Animals hide by staying inside.

Meet the Author and Illustrator

James Edward Arnosky

An acclaimed artist and naturalist, Arnosky observes nature while fishing, drawing, or walking.

"I write about the world I live in and try to share all I see and feel in my books," says Arnosky. He often describes the natural world in a way so that the reader becomes a part of the scene. He sums up the role of an author by saying, "The best nonfiction lets the reader knock on the door, and you let them in. Then you go away."

Theme Connections

Within the Selection

1. Why is it sometimes difficult to spot animals in a natural setting?

2. Why do animals need to hide?

Across Selections

3. How many different kinds of camouflage can you name?

Beyond the Selection

4. What other things can you think of that you have to look closely at to really see?

Write about It!

Describe an animal that changes color.

Remember to look for pictures of camouflaged animals to add to the **Concept/ Question Board.**

Science Inquiry

How Animals Hide

Many animals use a form of camouflage. Animals on land, in the air, and in the water use tricks to hide.

Land Animals

Many land animals use camouflage. Deer hide by using their coloration to blend in with their natural surroundings. The fur on a snowshoe hare changes to white in the winter. This helps it blend in with snow.

Animals in the Air

Camouflage is also used by animals that fly. Some butterflies use mimicry to scare away enemies. Owls and moths avoid harm by staying hidden on the bark of a tree.

Animals in the Water

Some animals that live in the water use camouflage. Some fish hide under rocks, and other fish have spots to make them look like rocks. Fish have clever ways of staying safe!

1. How is the heading for the last paragraph helpful?

2. How does the snowshoe hare hide from its enemies?

3. Compare the types of camouflage used by deer, moths, and fish. How are they the same? How are they different?

Try It!

As you work on your investigation, think about how you can use headings to organize your information.

How might grass help a rabbit to hide?
Why does a rabbit need to hide?

Rabbit

by Marilyn Singer
illustrated by Ken Robbins

watch me
            don't watch me
don't see me
            in the grass
pass me by
I'm a trick of the eye
don't chase
            just erase
what you see
one small smudge
            that won't budge
it's not me

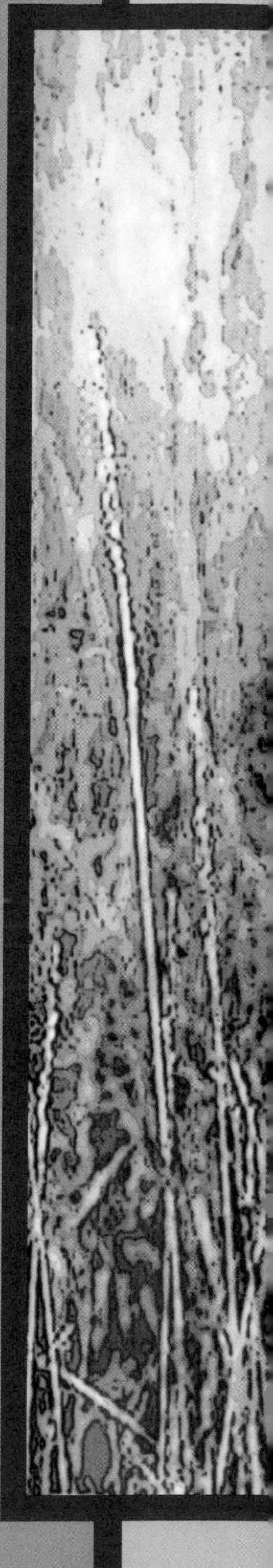

How does a tiger become an invisible hunter? Why does a tiger need to hide?

The Tiger

by Patricia M. Stockland

illustrated by Sara Rojo Pérez

The tiger
Hides in the
Early evening . . .

Teeth and claws and fur
Invisible hunter
Gold and black stripes hide him
Every inch silently creeping, then suddenly
Roaring, he pounces

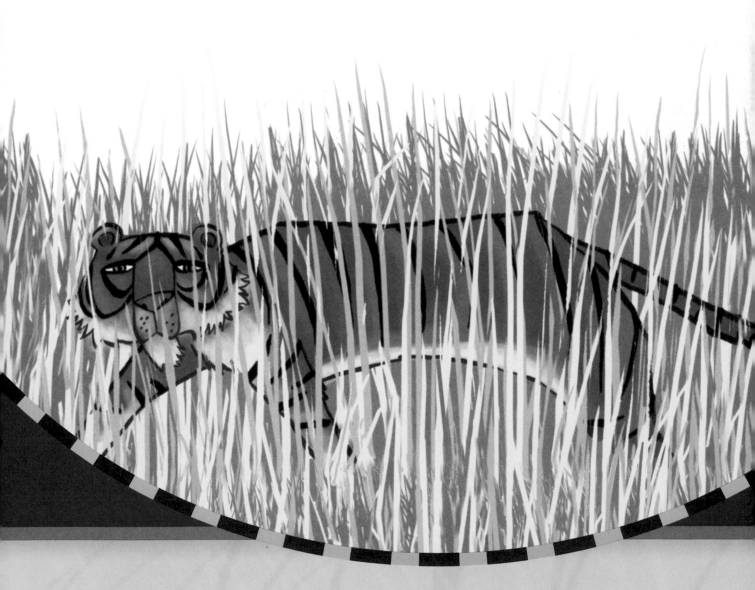

Test-Taking Strategy: Working Methodically

The best way to work on a test is to do one thing at a time. This is called working methodically.

Working Methodically

When you take a test, it might help to use these steps:

1. Read the question.

2. Read the answer choices.

3. Read the question again to be sure you understand it.

4. Pick the answer choice that you think is correct.

EXAMPLE

Try these four steps on the next question. Read this sentence:

In the cave, it was damp and cold.

1. What does the word *damp* mean in the sentence?

   ○ scary

   ○ wet

   ○ dark

When you use the four steps, you know the correct answer is *wet*.

Stripes

A large lion hid in the tall, yellow grass. It did not move. Its yellow fur helped it stay out of sight.

From its hiding spot, the lion watched a group of zebras. Their black-and-white stripes made them hard to see. The lion looked for a zebra standing alone.

As the lion watched, a young zebra stepped away from the group. In the tall grass, the lion started slinking toward the zebra. The zebra was unaware of the lion.

The sneaky lion carefully moved closer. The lion was trying to catch this young zebra.

Soon the lion was just yards from the zebra. The zebra still did not know the large lion was near.

153

Suddenly the lion charged at the young zebra! The young zebra saw the charging lion. All the zebras did. The young zebra ran toward the group. The zebras scrambled everywhere! They were afraid.

At first the lion kept running. But soon it could not tell where the young zebra was. All the lion could see was the moving black-and-white lines of the whole group. This hid the young zebra.

The lion ran back and forth. It did not see the young zebra. The lion stopped and watched as the group of zebras ran away.

The black-and-white stripes of the zebras helped hide the young zebra. The lion could not find it. The young zebra got away.

1. What animal hides in the tall, yellow grass?
- ◯ Tiger
- ◯ Zebra
- ◯ Deer
- ◯ Lion

2. In the story, what does the word *slinking* mean?
- ◯ roaring
- ◯ jumping
- ◯ standing
- ◯ creeping

3. How does the zebra get away from the lion?
- ◯ It hides behind a tree.
- ◯ It uses its black-and-white stripes.
- ◯ It changes colors.
- ◯ It hides in the tall, yellow grass.

4. What does the young zebra do when it sees the lion?
- ◯ It runs toward the lion.
- ◯ It runs toward the group of zebras.
- ◯ It hides behind a tree.
- ◯ It stands still.

5. Which of these happens last in the story?
- ◯ The zebras run away.
- ◯ The lion roars.
- ◯ The lion hides in the grass.
- ◯ The lion chases the zebra.

STOP

Courage

Do you have to be a hero to have courage? Or can courage mean giving an answer in class when you are not sure you are right? Maybe courage can be both of these things. What do you think?

Theme Connection

Look at the illustration.

- **What do you see?**

- **How do you think the girl at the microphone is feeling?**

- **How do you think the other children are feeling?**

Genre

Fantasy is a story that could not happen in the real world.

Comprehension Strategy

Making Connections
As you read, make connections between what you know and what you are reading.

Read the article to find the meanings of these words, which are also in "Dragons and Giants":

+ trembling
+ avalanche
+ leaping
+ puffing
+ afraid
+ brave

Vocabulary Strategy

Use **apposition** to find the meanings of *trembling* and *avalanche*.

Vocabulary
Warm-Up

A small rabbit sat under a fir tree at the base of a mountain. He was trembling, or shaking, with fear. An avalanche, snow and ice rolling down a mountain, just missed him.

As the rabbit was leaping away, he heard a soft puffing sound. Even though he was afraid, the rabbit decided to find out who made the noise. He looked all around, but he did not see anyone. He saw only white snow.

Then the rabbit heard someone cry out, "Please help me!"

He looked up and saw a mountain goat.

The goat was trying to hold on to a ledge of ice. "I am going to fall!" he called down.

"Do not worry! I will save you," shouted the rabbit. The rabbit used his back feet to make a big pile of snow under the ledge.

The snow pile was barely finished when the ledge broke. The goat landed gently in the snow.

"You are a brave rabbit," said the goat. "You knew there was danger, but you still helped me."

"It is easy being brave when you are helping a friend!" said the rabbit.

GAME

Sentence Building
Work with a partner to create sentences using the vocabulary words. Choose a word, and challenge your partner to make up a sentence using the word. Then switch roles. Continue until all the vocabulary words have been used.

Concept Vocabulary

The concept word for this lesson is **daring.** Someone who is *daring* is "willing to take or seek out risks." How did the rabbit show he was daring? Why does it take courage to be daring?

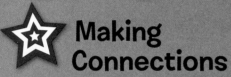

Fantasy is a story that could not happen in the real world.

Comprehension Strategy

⭐ **Making Connections**

As you read, make connections between what you know and what you are reading.

Focus Questions

Do you feel braver when you are with a friend? Does saying you are brave make you brave?

DRAGONS
and
GIANTS

by Arnold Lobel

Frog and Toad were reading a book together. "The people in this book are brave," said Toad. "They fight dragons and giants, and they are never afraid."

"I wonder if we are brave," said Frog. Frog and Toad looked into a mirror.

"We look brave," said Frog.

"Yes, but are we?" asked Toad.

Frog and Toad went outside.

"We can try to climb this mountain," said Frog. "That should tell us if we are brave."

Frog went leaping over rocks, and Toad came puffing up behind him.

They came to a dark cave. A big snake
came out of the cave.

"Hello lunch," said the snake when he saw
Frog and Toad. He opened his wide mouth.
Frog and Toad jumped away. Toad was
shaking.

"I am not afraid!" he cried.

They climbed higher, and they heard a loud noise. Many large stones were rolling down the mountain.

"It's an avalanche!" cried Toad. Frog and Toad jumped away. Frog was trembling.

"I am not afraid!" he shouted.

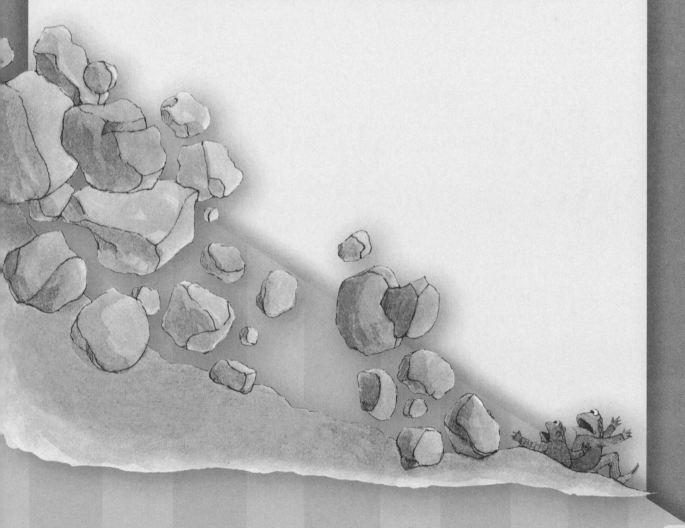

They came to the top of the mountain.
The shadow of a hawk fell over them. Frog
and Toad jumped under a rock. The hawk
flew away.

"We are not afraid!" screamed Frog and Toad at the same time. Then they ran down the mountain very fast. They ran past the place where they saw the avalanche. They ran past the place where they saw the snake. They ran all the way to Toad's house.

"Frog, I am glad to have a brave friend like you," said Toad. He jumped into the bed and pulled the covers over his head.

"And I am happy to know a brave person like you, Toad," said Frog. He jumped into the closet and shut the door.

Toad stayed in the bed, and Frog stayed in the closet.

They stayed there for a long time, just feeling very brave together.

Arnold Lobel

Lobel was often sick as a child, so he had a lot of time to look at books and to read. In the second-grade, he became known for his wonderful made-up stories. As he got older, his love for storytelling continued, and he also discovered a love of drawing. He illustrated a lot of books by other authors, but he also wrote many of his own books. Watching his children catch frogs and toads one summer gave him the idea to write some of his most popular books about characters with those names. Frog and Toad were special to Lobel because he used some of his own personality traits to create each of them.

Theme Connections

Within the Selection

1. Frog and Toad said they were not afraid. What do you think?

2. Do you think Frog and Toad proved they are brave? Why or why not?

Beyond the Selection

3. Have you ever done something to prove you were brave? What did you do?

4. Think about how "Dragons and Giants" adds to what you know about courage.

Write about It!

Describe a time when you were afraid but acted brave.

Remember to look for pictures and articles about courage to add to the **Concept/ Question Board.**

Science Inquiry

JOE'S INTERVIEW

Joe Cole wanted to write a school report about avalanches. Joe interviewed a ranger on the phone.

Joe: What is your name, and where do you work?

Ranger: My name is Raul Verde. I work in Rocky Mountain National Park. I measure changes in mountains over time. This helps us to better prepare for avalanches.

Joe: What is an avalanche?

Ranger: It is a huge mass of snow that moves at a great speed.

Joe: What usually causes an avalanche?

Ranger: Wind is the most common cause. Wind causes snow drifts. Snow drifts add weight. The weight of the snow drift causes the snow on the bottom to break. When this happens, snow falls like a waterfall.

Ranger: Most people don't know how loud an avalanche is.

Joe: Why are they loud?

Ranger: The falling snow vibrates to make a loud, deep sound.

Joe: How can I see an avalanche?

Ranger: Videos and photos are the best and safest ways to see an avalanche.

Think Link

1. Who talks first in this interview?
2. What causes the sound of an avalanche?
3. What is the most common cause of an avalanche?

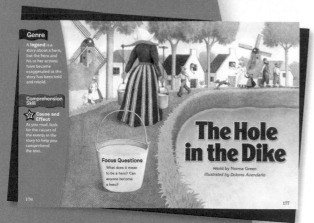

Read the article to find the meanings of these words, which are also in "The Hole in the Dike":

✦ **trickling**
✦ **flooded**
✦ **rumbling**
✦ **numb**
✦ **dikes**
✦ **windmills**

Vocabulary Strategy

Use **apposition** to find the meanings of *trickling* and *rumbling*.

Vocabulary

Warm-Up

Rain was trickling, or flowing drop by drop, down the window. Jin thought back to last June when her house flooded during a big thunderstorm.

Jin jumped at the sound of thunder that seemed to be rumbling, or making a heavy, deep rolling sound, through the walls. Jin went numb with fear. Then she heard her mother's calm voice.

"Come on, Jin," her mother called. "We need to move to higher ground."

As they were driving past the dikes, Jin heard a sound. At first she thought

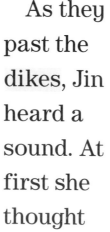

it was the water gurgling and gushing. Then she realized it was a dog howling.

"Stop the car, Mom!" begged Jin. "I hear dogs!"

"We need to keep moving," her mom said.

Jin looked out the window. Just past the windmills she saw a mother dog with her puppies. "Please stop," she said. "Those dogs are wet and scared."

Jin's mother turned the car around. They gathered up the frightened animals.

"The dogs will be safe and dry now," Jin said with a smile.

"I am sure the pups would thank you if they could," Jin's mother said.

Memory Game
Write each vocabulary word on an index card. Then write each word's meaning on its own card. Turn over and spread out the cards. Take turns with a partner matching each word with its meaning.

Concept Vocabulary

The concept word for this lesson is *responsible.* A person who is *responsible* is "able to be trusted or depended upon." Was Jin a responsible person? How did she show courage? Does it sometimes take courage to be responsible?

Genre

A **legend** is a story about a hero, but the hero and his or her actions have become exaggerated as the story has been told and retold.

Comprehension Skill

 Cause and Effect

As you read, look for the causes of the events in the story to help you comprehend the text.

Focus Questions

What does it mean to be a hero? Can anyone become a hero?

The Hole in the Dike

retold by Norma Green

illustrated by Dolores Avendaño

A long time ago, a boy named Peter
lived in Holland. He lived with his mother
and father in a cottage next to a tulip field.

Peter loved to look at the old windmills
turning slowly.

He loved to look at the sea.

In Holland, the land is very low, and the
sea is very high. The land is kept safe and
dry by high, strong walls called dikes.

179

One day Peter went to visit a friend who lived by the seaside.

As he started for home, he saw that the sun was setting and the sky was growing dark. "I must hurry or I shall be late for supper," said Peter.

"Take the short-cut along the top of the dike," his friend said.

They waved good-bye.

Peter wheeled his bike to the road on top of the dike. It had rained for several days, and the water looked higher than usual.

Peter thought, "It's lucky that the dikes are high and strong. Without these dikes, the land would be flooded and everything would be washed away."

Suddenly he heard a soft, gurgling noise. He saw a small stream of water trickling through a hole in the dike below.

Peter got off his bike to see what was wrong.

He couldn't believe his eyes. There in the big strong dike was a leak!

Peter slid down to the bottom of the dike. He put his finger in the hole to keep the water from coming through.

He looked around for help, but he could not see anyone on the road. He shouted. Maybe someone in the nearby field would hear him, he thought.

183

Only his echo answered. Everyone had gone home.

Peter knew that if he let the water leak through the hole in the dike, the hole would get bigger and bigger. Then the sea would come gushing through. The fields and the houses and the windmills would all be flooded.

Peter looked around for something to
plug up the leak so he could go to the
village for help.

He put a stone in the hole, then a stick.
But the stone and the stick were washed
away by the water.

Peter had to stay there alone. He had to use all his strength to keep the water out.

From time to time he called for help. But no one heard him.

All night long Peter kept his finger in the dike.

His fingers grew cold and numb. He wanted to sleep, but he couldn't give up.

At last, early in the morning, Peter heard
a welcome sound. Someone was coming! It
was the milk cart rumbling down the road.

Peter shouted for help. The milkman was
surprised to hear someone near that road
so early in the morning. He stopped and
looked around.

"Help!!" Peter shouted. "Here I am, at the bottom of the dike. There's a leak in the dike. Help! Help!"

The man saw Peter and hurried down to him. Peter showed him the leak and the little stream of water coming through.

Peter asked the milkman to hurry to the
village. "Tell the people. Ask them to send
some men to repair the dike right away!"

The milkman went as fast as he could.
Peter had to stay with his finger in the dike.

At last the men from the village came.
They set to work to repair the leak.

189

All the people thanked Peter. They carried him on their shoulders, shouting, "Make way for the hero of Holland! The brave boy who saved our land!"

But Peter did not think of himself as
a hero. He had done what he thought
was right. He was glad that he could do
something for the country he loved so
much.

Meet the Author

Norma Green

More than a hundred years ago, an American woman named Mary Mapes Dodge told this story of the dike to her children, making it up as she went along. Green said, "I felt there was a need today for young people to read about courage and pride in country. This story seemed to be a way of passing on these messages in a memorable fantasy."

Meet the Illustrator

Dolores Avendaño

Ever since Avendaño can remember, she wanted to become an illustrator. Her favorite part about being an illustrator is making dreams, fantasies, and stories seem real through her illustrations.

Theme Connections

Within the Selection

1. How did Peter find the courage to plug the hole in the dike?

2. Why did the people think Peter was a brave hero?

Across Selections

3. What other stories have you read that show courage?

Beyond the Selection

4. Whom do you consider a hero?

Write about It!

Describe a time you acted bravely because you knew it was the right thing to do.

Remember to add items about courage to the **Concept/Question Board.**

Hoover Dam Has Many Jobs

by Pedro Martina

Hoover Dam is 730 feet tall. It runs across the Colorado River. When the dam was built in the 1930s, it was called Boulder Dam. It was renamed for President Hoover in 1947.

Hoover Dam has four main jobs. One of its jobs is to prevent flooding. Water from the river used to flood the land. Today, the dam controls the water.

"Without the dam, people would be in danger," says Alice Batt, a Hoover Dam tour guide.

The dam also helps save water. This is important in case there is ever a drought.

"Hoover Dam supplies many cities in the area with water," says Batt.

The dam's fourth job is to produce power.

Batt says the dam is a good place to visit. Batt says the best part of visiting the dam is standing at the bottom and yelling. "You can hear your voice echo for two minutes!"

1. How does newspaper text look different from text in a book?

2. How does Hoover Dam help keep people safe?

3. What are Hoover Dam's four main jobs?

Try It!

As you work on your investigation, remember to look in newspaper articles for information.

Read the article to find the meanings of these words, which are also in "The Empty Pot":

- transferred
- sprout
- courage
- tended
- blossom
- kingdom
- emperor

Vocabulary Strategy

Use **context clues** to find the meanings of *transferred, sprout,* and *tended.*

Vocabulary
Warm-Up

Jose had been waiting for spring to arrive. But he wanted to stay in the country. He did not want to move to the city.

"I want to plant my garden in the country," exclaimed Jose.

"Many people are transferred and have to move to other places, just like us," said Jose's mom.

"It is hard to grow a garden in the city!" replied Jose.

"You have a green thumb, Jose. Your seeds will sprout and begin to grow," said Jose's mom. "You can have a beautiful garden in the city."

The move was hard for Jose. One day his mother had an idea. "Talk to the manager of our building," she said. "He might let you plant a garden by the front door."

Jose was afraid the manager would not let him plant his garden. It took a week for Jose to work up the courage to talk to the manager, but he finally did.

"A garden is a great idea, Jose," said the manager. "Our building will look beautiful."

Jose planted his garden. He watched over and tended his garden every day. Soon the flowers began to blossom. His building looked like a kingdom fit for an emperor. Jose was proud. He felt like the emperor of his building!

GAME

Guessing Game
Choose a partner. Ask your partner, "What word means 'to bloom'?" After correctly guessing *blossom*, it is your partner's turn to choose a word for you to guess. Review all the vocabulary words.

Concept Vocabulary

The concept word for this lesson is *fear*. *Fear* means "to be worried or anxious." What was Jose worried or anxious about?

A **folktale** is a story that has been passed down from generation to generation through an oral tradition before it was written down.

Comprehension Strategy

☆ **Predicting** As you read, predict what you think will happen next in the story. Confirm or revise your predictions as you continue to read the story.

The Empty Pot

by Demi

Focus Questions

Why does it take courage to tell the truth? Does it take courage to admit failure?

A long time ago in China there was a
boy named Ping who loved flowers.
Anything he planted burst into bloom. Up
came flowers, bushes, and even big fruit
trees, as if by magic!

Everyone in the kingdom loved flowers
too. They planted them everywhere, and
the air smelled like perfume.

The Emperor loved birds and animals, but flowers most of all, and he tended his own garden every day. But the Emperor was very old. He needed to choose a successor to the throne.

Who would his successor be? And how would the Emperor choose? Because the Emperor loved flowers so much, he decided to let the flowers choose.

201

The next day a proclamation was issued:
All the children in the land were to come
to the palace. There they would be given
special flower seeds by the Emperor.
"Whoever can show me their best in a
year's time," he said, "will succeed me to
the throne."

This news created great excitement throughout the land! Children from all over the country swarmed to the palace to get their flower seeds. All the parents wanted their children to be chosen Emperor, and all the children hoped they would be chosen too!

203

When Ping received his seed from the Emperor, he was the happiest child of all. He was sure he could grow the most beautiful flower.

Ping filled a flowerpot with rich soil. He planted the seed in it very carefully.

He watered it
every day. He
couldn't wait to
see it sprout, grow,
and blossom into a
beautiful flower!

Day after day
passed, but nothing
grew in his pot.

205

Ping was very worried. He put new soil into a bigger pot. Then he transferred the seed into the rich black soil.

Another two months he waited. Still nothing happened.

By and by the whole year passed.

Spring came, and all the children put on their best clothes to greet the Emperor.

They rushed to the palace with their beautiful flowers, eagerly hoping to be chosen.

207

Ping was ashamed of his empty pot. He thought the other children would laugh at him because for once he couldn't get a flower to grow.

His clever friend ran by, holding a great big plant. "Ping!" he said. "You're not really going to the Emperor with an empty pot, are you? Couldn't you grow a great big flower like mine?"

"I've grown lots of flowers better than yours," Ping said. "It's just this seed that won't grow."

Ping's father overheard this and said, "You did your best, and your best is good enough to present to the Emperor."

Holding the empty pot in his hands, Ping went straight away to the palace.

The Emperor was looking at the flowers slowly, one by one.

How beautiful all the flowers were!

But the Emperor was frowning and did not say a word.

Finally he came to Ping. Ping hung his head in shame, expecting to be punished.

The Emperor asked him, "Why did you bring an empty pot?"

Ping started to cry and replied, "I planted the seed you gave me and I watered it every day, but it didn't sprout. I put it in a better pot with better soil, but still it didn't sprout! I tended it all year long, but nothing grew. So today I had to bring an empty pot without a flower. It was the best I could do."

When the Emperor heard these words, a smile slowly spread over his face, and he put his arm around Ping. Then he exclaimed to one and all, "I have found him! I have found the one person worthy of being Emperor!

"Where you got your seeds from, I do not know. For the seeds I gave you had all been cooked. So it was impossible for any of them to grow.

"I admire Ping's great courage to appear before me with the empty truth, and now I reward him with my entire kingdom and make him Emperor of all the land!"

Meet the Author and Illustrator

Charlotte Dumaresq Hunt

Hunt uses her childhood nickname, Demi, as her pen name. She studied art in several schools, but much of her learning took place as she traveled. She has been to faraway places such as Brazil, India, and China. Some of the things she learned and saw while in China are seen in "The Empty Pot."

She has not limited her art to children's books. Many of her paintings and prints hang in museums in the United States and India. She has also painted wall murals in Mexico and the dome of a church in California.

Theme Connections

Within the Selection

1. Ping was ashamed of his empty pot. Why did he present it to the Emperor anyway?

2. How did the Emperor know Ping deserved to be Emperor?

Across Selections

3. Were you surprised by the ending? Why? Did any other stories we have read surprise you at the end? Explain.

Beyond the Selection

4. Have you ever needed courage when you thought your best was not good enough?

Write about It!

Describe a time when you had to find the courage to be honest.

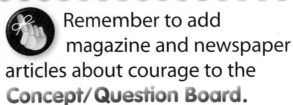

Remember to add magazine and newspaper articles about courage to the **Concept/Question Board.**

Window Gardens

Some people do not have a lot of space outside to grow a garden. They grow a window garden instead.

Window gardens are planted in long boxes. The boxes must have holes in the bottom so water can drain. Just like outdoor gardens, window gardens need sunlight and water.

Springtime Flowers

Pansies can grow well in window boxes. They have colorful flowers. They bloom only in the spring though.

Summertime Flowers

Some people like flowers to blossom all summer. Petunias make good summer plants for window boxes. Plant a petunia seed, and watch it bloom all summer long. Each tiny seed will become a new plant.

Their colorful blossoms can brighten any room.

Window gardens are fun and pretty. All they need is water, sun, and a little care from you!

Think Link

1. How is the heading for the third paragraph helpful?

2. Why might someone grow a window garden?

3. Name one flower that can grow in a window box.

Try It!

As you work on your investigation, think about how you could use headings to organize your information.

AKIAK
A Tale from the Iditarod
by Robert J. Blake

AKIAK

Focus Questions
Do you think animals can be courageous? In what ways?

220   221

Read the article to find the meanings of these words, which are also in "Akiak: A Tale from the Iditarod":

✦ rumble
✦ rugged
✦ snowdrift
✦ burrowed
✦ squinted
✦ shifted
✦ snapped

Vocabulary Strategy

Use **word structure** to determine the meanings of *burrowed, squinted, shifted,* and *snapped.*

Vocabulary

Warm-Up

The rumble of the snow echoed. Joe and Juan had made it down the rugged, or rough and uneven, mountain. They were still trying to reach the van that held the ski team.

Joe looked back up at the steep mountain that glistened in the moonlight. "There is no point in racing to the road. A big snowdrift is in the way," he said.

Juan agreed. They burrowed, or dug, into the snow. The stillness of the night lulled them to a restless sleep. Juan and Joe woke with the early morning sun.

Juan squinted. The sunshine on the snow was almost blinding. When his eyes adjusted to the brightness, he saw endless white. "That snowdrift is huge. It is going to be hard getting out of here," he said.

Joe shifted his body in the snow. "I know the ski team will figure out a way to help us!" he said.

The words were no sooner out of Joe's mouth when they heard the sound of a motor. Joe and Juan snapped to attention.

A big snowplow appeared. It moved the snowdrift as though it were as light as a feather.

GAME

Fill In the Blank
On a sheet of paper, use each of the vocabulary words in a sentence. Draw a blank line in place of the vocabulary word in each sentence. Give your paper to another student. Have your partner fill in each blank with the correct vocabulary word.

Concept Vocabulary

The concept word for this lesson is **danger.** *Danger* is "something that may cause harm or injury." What danger did Juan and Joe face? How does having courage help you face danger?

219

Realistic Fiction is a story that did not happen, but the characters, places, and events in the story seem real.

Comprehension Skill

☆ **Sequence** As you read, pay attention to the order in which the events in the story take place.

AKIAK

A Tale from the Iditarod

by Robert J. Blake

221

DAY ONE

Akiak knew it. The other dogs knew it, too.

Some had run it many times and others had never run it at all. But not a dog wanted to be left behind.

It was Iditarod Race Day. 1,151 miles of wind, snow, and rugged trail lay ahead, from Anchorage to Nome. Akiak had led the team through seven races and knew the trail better than any dog. She had brought them in fifth, third, and second, but had never won. She was ten years old now. This was her last chance. Now, they must win now.

Crack! The race was under way. One by one, fifty-eight teams took off for Nome.

DAY TWO

"Come on, old girl, show 'em how," Mick called. "Haw!"

Mick worked the sixteen-dog team through Akiak, calling "Haw!" when she needed the dogs to turn left, and "Gee!" to go right. Mick was the musher, but the team followed the lead dog. The team followed Akiak.

Through steep climbs and dangerous descents, icy waters and confusing trails, Akiak always found the safest and fastest way. She never got lost.

DAY THREE

Akiak and Squinty, Big Boy and Flinty, Roscoe and the rest of the team pounded across the snow for three days. The dogs were ready to break out, but Mick held them back. There was a right time—but not yet.

High in the Alaskan range they caught up to Willy Ketcham in third place. It was his team that had beaten them by just one minute last year. Following the rules, Willy pulled over and allowed Mick's team to pass.

"That old dog will never make it!" he laughed at Akiak across the biting wind.

"She'll be waiting for you at Nome!" Mick vowed.

DAY FOUR

High in the Kuskokwim Mountains they passed Tall Tim Broonzy's team and moved into second place. Just after Takotna, Mick's team made its move. They raced by Whistlin' Perry's team to take over first place.

Ketcham made his move, too. His team clung to Mick's like a shadow.

Akiak and her team now had to break trail through deep snow. It was tough going. By the Ophir checkpoint, Akiak was limping. The deep snow had jammed up one of her pawpads and made it sore. Mick tended to her as Ketcham raced by and took first place from them.

"You can't run on that paw, old girl," Mick said to her. "With a day's rest it will heal, but the team can't wait here a day. We've got to go on without you. You'll be flown home."

Roscoe took Akiak's place at lead.

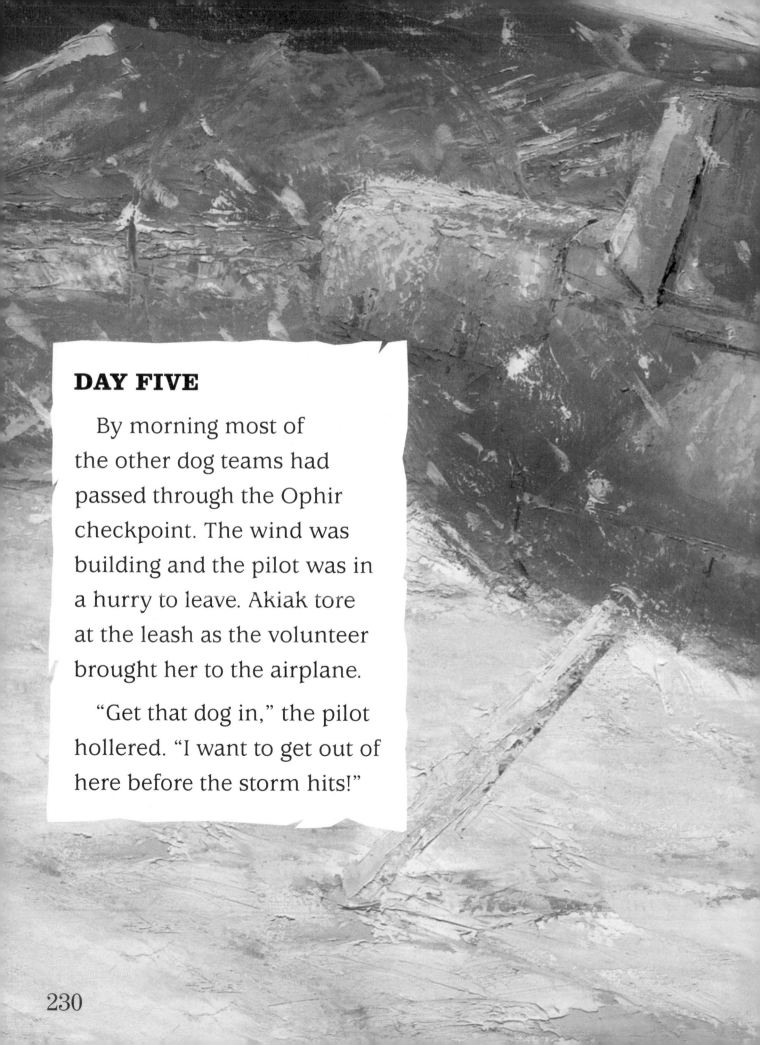

DAY FIVE

By morning most of the other dog teams had passed through the Ophir checkpoint. The wind was building and the pilot was in a hurry to leave. Akiak tore at the leash as the volunteer brought her to the airplane.

"Get that dog in," the pilot hollered. "I want to get out of here before the storm hits!"

Akiak jumped and pulled and snapped. All she wanted was to get back on the trail. To run. To win. Then all at once, the wind gusted, the plane shifted, and Akiak twisted out of the handler's grip. By the time they turned around she was gone.

232

DAY SIX

Akiak ran while the storm became a blizzard. She knew that Mick and the team were somewhere ahead of her. The wind took away the scent and the snow took away the trail, but still she knew the way. She ran and she ran, until the blizzard became a whiteout. Then she could run no more. While Mick and the team took refuge in Galena, seven hours ahead, Akiak burrowed into a snowdrift to wait out the storm.

In the morning the mound of snow came alive, and out pushed Akiak.

DAY SEVEN

Word had gone out that Akiak was loose. Trail volunteers knew that an experienced lead dog would stick to the trail. They knew she'd have to come through Unalakleet.

She did. Six hours after Mick and the team had left, Akiak padded softly, cautiously, into the checkpoint. Her ears alert, her wet nose sniffed the air. The team had been there, she could tell.

Suddenly, cabin doors flew open. Five volunteers fanned out and tried to grab her. Akiak zigged around their every zag and took off down the trail.

"Call ahead to Shaktoolik!" a man shouted.

235

DAY EIGHT

At Shaktoolik, Mick dropped two more dogs and raced out, still six hours ahead of Akiak.

Hungry now—it had been two days since she had eaten—Akiak pounded over the packed trail. For thirst, she drank out of the streams, the ice broken through by the sled teams.

She struggled into Shaktoolik in the late afternoon. Three men spotted her and chased her right into the community hall, where some mushers were sleeping. Tables overturned and coffee went flying. Then one musher opened the back door and she escaped.

"Go find them, girl," he whispered.

At Koyuk, Akiak raided the mushers' discard pile for food. No one came after her. At Elim, people put food out for her. Almost everybody was rooting for Akiak to catch her team.

DAY NINE

Mick rushed into White Mountain twenty-two minutes behind Ketcham. Here the teams had to take an eight-hour layover to rest before the final dash for Nome. Mick dropped Big Boy and put young Comet in his place. The team was down to eight dogs with seventy-seven miles to go.

Akiak pushed on. When her team left White Mountain at 6 P.M., Akiak was running through Golovin, just two hours behind. A crowd lined the trail to watch her run through the town.

DAY TEN

Screaming winds threw bitter cold at the team as they fought their way along the coast. Then, halfway to the checkpoint called Safety, they came upon a maze of snowmobile tracks. The lead dogs lost the trail.

Mick squinted through the snow, looking for a sign.

There. Going right. She recognized Ketcham's trail.

"Gee!" she called. Gee—go right.

But the dogs wouldn't go. They wandered about, tangling up the lines. Mick straightened them out and worked the team up the hill. At the top they stopped short. Something was blocking the trail.

241

"Akiak!" Mick called.

She ran to her usual spot at the harness, waiting to be hooked in.

"Sorry, old girl." Mick hugged her. "Rules say I can't put you back in harness. Get in the sled."

But instead, Akiak circled the lead dogs, pushing them and barking.

"What is it, girl?" Mick asked.

Akiak ran back down the hill.

Mick laughed. Ketcham's team had taken the wrong trail! She turned her team around and rushed them down to Akiak, who jumped into the sled.

"Take us to Nome!" Mick called to her.

Mick first heard the noise a mile outside
of Nome. At first she wasn't sure what it
was. It grew so loud that she couldn't hear
the dogs. It was a roar, or a rumble—she
was so tired after ten days of mushing
she couldn't tell which. Then she saw the
crowd and she heard the cheers. People
had come from everywhere to see the
courageous dog that had run the Iditarod
trail alone.

As sure as if she had been in the lead position, Akiak won the Iditarod Race.

"Nothing was going to stop this dog from winning," Mick told the crowd. Akiak knew it.

The other dogs knew it, too.

Robert J. Blake

Blake always wanted to be an artist. When he was in school, he made comic strips for his friends to read. He even painted his first oil painting when he was only fourteen years old. It is important for Blake to paint directly from real life, so he uses his memories and his travels to create his illustrations. For "Akiak: A Tale from the Iditarod," Blake witnessed an Iditarod race firsthand.

Theme Connections

Within the Selection

1. How did Akiak show courage?

2. Did anyone else in the story show courage?

Across Selections

3. How is "Akiak: A Tale from the Iditarod" different from the other stories in this unit?

Beyond the Selection

4. How might the story have ended if Akiak had not been brave and found her team?

5. Think about how "Akiak: A Tale from the Iditarod" adds to what you know about courage.

Write about It!

Describe a time when you have seen an animal acting courageous.

Remember to look for pictures of courageous animals to add to the **Concept/ Question Board.**

Bulldozers

In the 1800s, *bulldozing* was a common term. It meant "to use force to push over or through any object."

Bulldozers are machines that do just that. Some bulldozers can weigh **seventy** tons. That is a big machine!

Some bulldozers level land. They make way for houses and shopping centers. Other bulldozers break through the earth and rocks.

A bulldozer has two main tools. The **ripper** is the long part on the back of the bulldozer. It looks like a claw. The ripper can break through rocks and hard dirt.

The **blade** is a heavy metal plate. It is on the front of the bulldozer. It can push through things.

Bulldozers are important machines. They can push over or through most things!

1. How is the bold print in this story helpful?

2. What are the two main tools on a bulldozer?

3. How does each tool work?

Try It!

As you work on your unit investigation, remember to use bold and italic text to emphasize words.

Read the article to find the meanings of these words, which are also in "Brave as a Mountain Lion":

- ✦ reservation
- ✦ dreaded
- ✦ qualified
- ✦ mysterious
- ✦ mountain lion
- ✦ stomping
- ✦ inform

Vocabulary Strategy

Use **apposition** to find the meanings of *qualified, stomping,* and *inform.*

Vocabulary

Warm-Up

Luyu was as graceful as the birds in the sky. "That is why I named you Luyu," her mother told her. "*Luyu* means 'wild dove.'"

Luyu liked to explore the woods. Her mother warned her not to stray from the reservation by herself. Luyu dreaded each talk because she felt qualified, or able, to go out by herself.

One day Luyu heard a mysterious sound. She looked out the window. A mountain lion was stomping, or walking heavily, in the snow. It was stalking a hurt dove.

"I must do something," thought Luyu. But Luyu knew she should not go into the woods by herself.

Luyu ran to inform, or tell, her mother about the mountain lion. Luyu's mother made a loud noise. The startled lion ran away.

Luyu and her mother wrapped the dove in a blanket. Luyu took care of the dove.

One bright sunny morning Luyu and her mother walked into the woods. With tears in her eyes, Luyu released the dove. She watched it fly into the blue sky.

GAME

Flash Cards
Make a set of flash cards with the vocabulary words. Write the word on one side and its definition on the other side. Use the flash cards to review the vocabulary words and definitions. Then ask a partner to use the cards to quiz you.

Concept Vocabulary

The concept word for this lesson is **advice.** *Advice* is "an idea about how to solve a problem or how to act in a certain situation." What advice did Luyu's mother give her about going into the woods? Did it take courage for Luyu to follow her mother's advice? Why or why not?

BRAVE AS A MOUNTAIN LION

by **Ann Herbert Scott**

illustrated by ***Glo Coalson***

Focus Questions

Why do we need to have the courage to stand up to our fears? Have you ever had a fear of standing up in front of an audience?

It was snowing hard. Pressing his face against the cold glass of the living room window, Spider could barely see his father's horses crowding against the fence. Soon the reservation would be covered with darkness.

Spider shivered. Any other night he would have been hoping his father would reach home before the snow drifted too high to push through. But tonight was different. Tonight he dreaded his father's coming.

In his pocket Spider could feel two pieces of paper from school. One he wanted to show his father. One he didn't. Not tonight. Not ever.

Beside him on the couch his sister Winona was playing with her doll. Lucky kid, thought Spider. Winona was too little to worry about anything, especially school.

Just then Spider saw the blinking red
lights of the snowplow clearing the road
beside their house. Right behind came his
father's new blue pickup. Spider sighed. At
least Dad was home safe. Now the trouble
would begin!

Winona ran to the back door. But Spider
stayed on the couch, waiting. From the
kitchen he could smell dinner cooking. His
favorite, deer meat. But tonight he didn't
even feel like eating. Soon he heard the
sound of his father and his brother Will
stomping the snow from their boots.

Spider's father came in with an armful of mail from the post office. He hung up his hat and jacket on the pegs by the kitchen and stretched out in his favorite chair.

"So what did you do in school today?" he asked Spider.

"Not much," said Spider, feeling his pocket.

"Did you bring home any papers?"

Spider nodded. How did his father always know?

"Let's take a look," said his father.

Spider took the first paper from his pocket. "Here's the good one," he said.

"Spelling one hundred percent. Every word correct. Good for you, son."

"But, Dad, I'm in trouble." Spider shoved the other paper into his father's hand. "The teacher wants me to be in the big school spelling bee."

Spider's father read out loud: "Dear Parent, I am pleased to inform you that your son Spider has qualified for the school spelling bee, which will be held next Thursday night. We hope you and your family will attend."

Spider's mother and grandmother came in from the kitchen with the platter of deer meat and bowls of beans and corn for dinner. "That's a good report, Little Brother," his grandmother said, smiling.

"But I won't do it," said Spider.

"Why not?" asked Will.

"I'm too afraid," said Spider.

"But you're a brave boy," said his father. "Why are you afraid?"

"Dad," said Spider, "you have to stand high up on the stage in the gym and all the people look at you. I'm afraid my legs would freeze together and I wouldn't be able to walk. And if I did get up there, no sound would come out when I opened my mouth. It's too scary."

"Oh, I see," said his father.

Spider's mother put her hand on his shoulder. "You must be hungry. Let's eat."

After dinner Spider sat by the wood stove doing his homework. "Dad, were you ever in a spelling bee?" he asked.

"As a matter of fact, I was."

"Were you scared?"

"I was very scared. I didn't even want to do it. But then my father told me to pretend I was a brave animal, the strongest, bravest animal I could think of. Then I wasn't afraid anymore."

Later, Spider sat up in bed thinking of animals who weren't afraid of anything. Above his head hung the picture of a mountain lion his dad had painted for him. How about a mountain lion, the King of the Beasts?

Spider took his flashlight from under his pillow and shined its beam on the face of the great wild creature. "Brave as a mountain lion," he said to himself in a loud, strong voice.

"Brave as a mountain lion," he repeated in his mind as he was falling asleep.

"I'll try to be brave as a mountain lion," he whispered to his father the next morning as he brushed his hair for school.

At recess the next day Spider peeked into the gymnasium. The huge room was empty. He looked up at the mural painting of the western Shoshone people of long ago. They were brave hunters of deer and antelope and elk, just as his father and his uncles were today.

At the far end of the gym was the scoreboard with the school's emblem, the eagle. Every Saturday in the winter Spider and his whole family came to cheer for Will and the basketball team. Those players weren't afraid of anything.

Then Spider stared up at the stage. That's where the spellers would stand. He could feel his throat tighten and hear his heart thumping, bumpity-bumpity-bumpity-bump. How could he ever get up there in front of all the people? Spider ran outside, slamming the gym door behind him.

That afternoon it was still snowing. At home Spider found his grandmother beading a hatband for his father's birthday. Spider watched her dip her needle into the bowls of red and black and white beads.

"Grandma, were you ever in a spelling bee?"

"No, I never was," his grandmother answered. "Are you thinking much about it?"

"All the time," said Spider.

"What's the worst part?"

"Being up on the stage with all the people looking at you."

"Oh, that's easy," said his grandmother. "You can be clever. Clever as a coyote. The coyote always has some trick to help him out of trouble. When you're up there on the stage, you don't have to look at the people. You can turn your back on them and pretend they aren't even there."

In bed that night Spider pulled the covers over his head. "Brave as a mountain lion, clever as a coyote," he kept repeating to himself as he fell asleep.

The next morning Spider scraped a peephole in the ice on his bedroom window. He couldn't see the far mountains for the swirling snow. He smiled as he packed his book bag. If it kept snowing like this, maybe the principal would close school tomorrow.

In class that day all everybody could talk about was the spelling bee. "Can we count on you, Spider?" asked Miss Phillips, his teacher.

Spider shook his head. "Maybe," he said. "I haven't made up my mind."

"You'd better make up your mind soon," said Miss Phillips. "The spelling bee is tomorrow night."

After lunch Spider walked by the gym door, but this time he didn't open it. He didn't have to. He remembered just how everything looked. Scary. When he thought about it, a shiver went all the way down his spine.

By the afternoon the snow had piled in drifts higher than Spider's head. Spider got a bowl of popcorn and went to the carport to watch Will shoot baskets. Time after time the ball slipped through the net. Will almost never missed.

"How about some popcorn for me?" Will asked his little brother. Spider brought back another bowl from the kitchen.

"Are you practicing for the spelling bee?" asked Will.

"I've decided not to be in it," said Spider. "I'm going to be brave when I'm bigger."

Will nodded. "I remember those spelling bees."

"Were you afraid?" asked Spider.

"I was scared silly," said Will. "I was so scared I was afraid I'd wet my pants. Then I learned the secret."

"What's the secret?" asked Spider.

"To be silent."

"Silent?" asked Spider. "What does that do?"

"It keeps you cool. When I have a hard shot to make and the whole team depends on me, that's when I get very silent."

Spider didn't say anything. He just watched his brother shooting one basket after another. Then he saw her. High above the shelves of paint and livestock medicines was a tiny insect. It was his old friend, Little Spider, dangling on a long strand as she spun a new part of her web. She was silent. Silent as the moon.

Spider laughed. How could he have forgotten! Grandmother often told him how when he was a baby in his cradle board he used to watch for hours while a little spider spun her web above his head. She had been his first friend. Ever since, his family had called him Spider.

Taking the stepladder, Spider climbed up close so he could watch the tiny creature. How brave she was, dropping down into space with nothing to hang onto. And how clever, weaving a web out of nothing but her own secret self. "Say something," he whispered.

The little insect was silent. But Spider felt she was talking to him in her own mysterious way. "Listen to your spirit," she seemed to say. "Listen to your spirit and you'll never be afraid."

The next morning the snow had stopped. Outside Spider's window icicles glistened in the sun. No chance of school being closed today.

"Brave as a mountain lion, clever as a coyote, silent as a spider," Spider thought to himself as he buttoned his vest.

Winona pushed open the door. "Are you going to do it?"

"I'm going to do it," Spider answered.

That night all the family came, his grandmother who lived with them and his other grandparents and his father and his mother and three aunts and two uncles and Will and Winona and lots of their cousins. Three of his cousins were going to be in the spelling bee, too.

Brave as a mountain lion, Spider climbed up the steps to the stage. Clever as a coyote, he turned his back so he wouldn't see the rows of people down below. Silently, he listened to his spirit. Bumpity-bump-bump went his heart.

All the best spellers in his class were up there on the stage, standing in a line. The principal gave them the words, one by one.

At first the words were easy. "Yellow," said the principal. "I have a yellow dog."

Spider kept his eyes on the principal's face. "Yellow," said Spider. "Y-e-l-l-o-w. Yellow."

"Correct," said the principal.

Then the words got a little harder. "February," said the principal. "Soon it will be February." It was Spider's turn again.

"February," said Spider, remembering the *r*. "Capital f-e-b-r-u-a-r-y. February."

"Correct," said the principal.

Finally there were only two spellers left standing—Spider and Elsie, a girl from the other side of the reservation.

"Terrific," said the principal. "We have a terrific basketball team."

"Terrific," said Spider, taking a big breath. "T-e-r-r-i-f-f-i-c. Terrific."

"Incorrect," said the principal. Then she turned to Elsie. "Terrific. We have a terrific basketball team."

"Terrific," said Elsie. "T-e-r-r-i-f-i-c. Terrific."

"Correct," said the principal. "Let's give a hand to our two winners from Miss Phillips' class: Elsie in first place and Spider in second place."

It was over! Spider climbed down the steps and found the rows where his family were sitting. Spider's father shook his hand and Will slapped him on the back. "You did it!" his mother said proudly. "You stood right up there in front of everybody!"

"It was easy," said Spider.

"You were brave," said his father. "Brave as a mountain lion."

"And clever," said his grandmother. "Clever as a coyote."

I wasn't even afraid, Spider thought. I listened to my spirit. "But now I'm hungry," he told his family. "Hungry as a bear. Let's all go home and eat."

Meet the Author

Ann Herbert Scott

Scott talks a lot with children to see what they think about her ideas. When speaking about this story, she said, "The story idea came directly from a boy who was confronted by an everyday challenge to his courage: his fear of standing up before an audience as part of the annual school spelling bee."

Meet the Illustrator

Glo Coalson

Coalson created her first book from Eskimo folktales she had collected while in Alaska. Since then, she has illustrated more than twenty children's books. She uses watercolors, pastels, and ink to create her illustrations.

Courage

Theme Connections

Within the Selection

1. Why was Spider afraid to be in the spelling bee?

2. How was Spider able to overcome his fear?

Across Selections

3. What was Ping afraid of in "The Empty Pot"? What was Spider afraid of? How were their fears alike or different?

Beyond the Selection

4. When have you been afraid to do something? What helped you overcome your fear?

Write about It!

Describe a time when you overcame your fear to do something.

Remember to add pictures and articles about courage to the **Concept/Question Board.**

Homes of Native Americans

Many years ago, Native Americans lived in many different types of homes. The type of home was different for each region of the country.

In the Northwest, Native Americans lived in plank houses made from wood. A plank house had a V-shaped roof.

On the West Coast, Native Americans made conical houses. They used tree poles and tied them together with vines.

Teepees were used on the Plains. A teepee was made with long poles that were covered with animal skins. Teepees could be taken apart easily to move to another reservation.

In the Northeast, Native Americans lived in long houses. Elm tree trunks were used to build the long houses. Many people lived in the same long house.

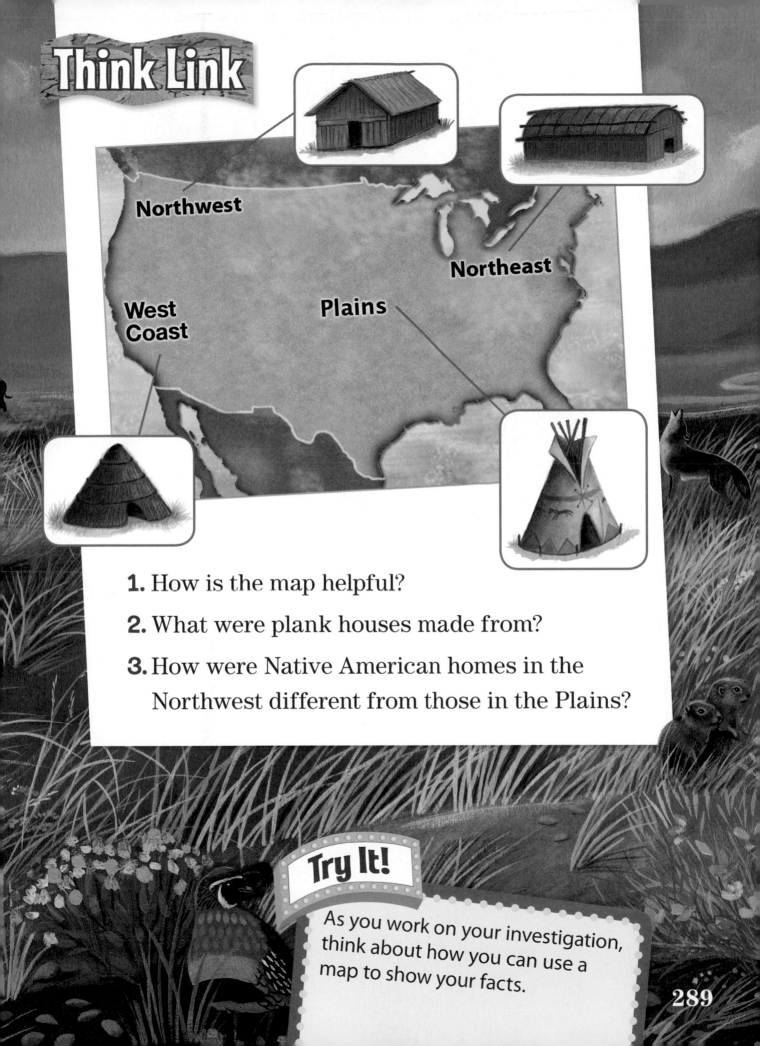

Northwest

Northeast

West Coast

Plains

1. How is the map helpful?

2. What were plank houses made from?

3. How were Native American homes in the Northwest different from those in the Plains?

Try It!

As you work on your investigation, think about how you can use a map to show your facts.

Focus Questions
What frightens you?
What do you do to
overcome your fears?

LIFE
DOESN'T
FRIGHTEN ME

by Maya Angelou

illustrated by Jana Christy

Shadows on the wall
Noises down the hall
Life doesn't frighten me at all
Bad dogs barking loud
Big ghosts in a cloud
Life doesn't frighten me at all.

Mean old Mother Goose
Lions on the loose
They don't frighten me at all
Dragons breathing flame
On my counterpane
That doesn't frighten me at all.

I go boo
Make them shoo
I make fun
Way they run
I won't cry
So they fly
I just smile
They go wild
Life doesn't frighten me at all.

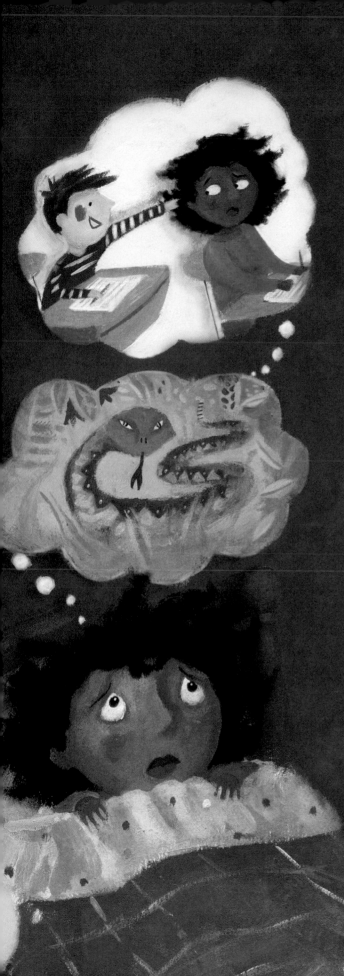

Tough guys in a fight
All alone at night
Life doesn't frighten me at all.
Panthers in the park
Strangers in the dark
No, they don't frighten me at all.

That new classroom where
Boys all pull my hair
(Kissy little girls
With their hair in curls)
They don't frighten me at all.

Don't show me frogs and snakes
And listen for my scream.
If I'm afraid at all
It's only in my dreams.

I've got a magic charm
That I keep up my sleeve,
I can walk the ocean floor
And never have to breathe.

Life doesn't frighten me at all
Not at all
Not at all
Life doesn't frighten me at all.

Focus Questions

Does it take courage to do the right thing?
Why does it take so much courage to say "no" when
we really want to say "yes" to our friends?

COURAGE

by Emily Hearn

illustrated by Kathryn Mitter

Courage is when you're allergic to cats and your new friend says can you come to her house to play after school and stay to dinner then maybe go skating and sleep overnight? And, she adds, you can pet her small kittens! Oh, how you ache to. It takes courage to say "no" to all that.

Test-Taking Strategy: Referring to a Story to Answer Questions

To answer some questions on a test, you may have to read a story. You must use the information in the story to answer each question.

Referring to a Story to Answer Questions

Sometimes you will read a story on a test. You do not have to memorize the story. You should look back at the story to answer the questions.

EXAMPLE

Read this story. Use the story to choose the best answer.

Nick is a big, brown dog. He has floppy ears. Nick likes to chase balls and do tricks.

1. What color is Nick?
  ○ brown
  ○ black
  ○ white

To answer the question, look back at the story. The story tells you that Nick is a *brown* dog. So the first answer is correct.

The Rescue

The small stream went through the town. It was usually just a few inches deep. Tiny fish swam in the stream. Frogs and turtles lived in it too.

People enjoyed walking beside the stream. It made a nice sound as it tumbled over the rocks. No one in the town ever worried about the stream. It was like an old friend.

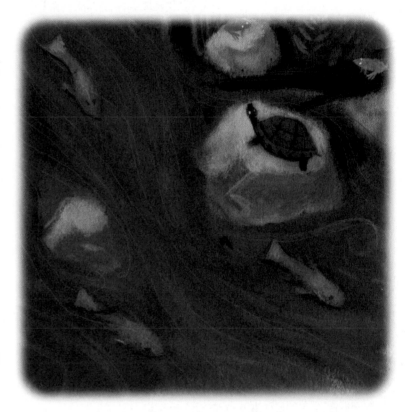

Late one summer day, rain started to fall. At first, people welcomed the rain. It would be good for the lawns and gardens. When people went to bed, the sound of the rain helped them sleep.

The rain fell all night. By the next morning, the stream was roaring over its banks. Many people came to see how their little stream had grown. Mayor Timms was worried.

GO ON

"Frankie, do not let Cody get too close. That water is really deep." Frankie's mother waved her arm to make the dog move back.

Just then, the bank started to crumble. Cody slid into the water.

Officer Pierce was standing just a few feet away. In a flash, she jumped into the water and grabbed Cody's collar. Officer Pierce and Cody struggled to the bank. Dozens of hands helped pull them out.

Everyone around them clapped when they saw that Cody and Officer Pierce were safe. Before long, the whole town would know how brave Officer Pierce had been.

1. Who tells Frankie not to let his dog get too close to the water?

- ◯ Officer Pierce
- ◯ His father
- ◯ Mayor Timms
- ◯ His mother

2. Which of these animals is <u>not</u> mentioned in the story?

- ◯ Fish
- ◯ Snake
- ◯ Frog
- ◯ Turtle

3. Which word in the story describes a sound?

- ◯ roaring
- ◯ waved
- ◯ standing
- ◯ helped

4. When the rain starts, people are happy because _____.

- ◯ the stream is too deep
- ◯ it is good for gardens
- ◯ the fish need a bigger stream
- ◯ the summer is hot

5. How does Officer Pierce save Cody?

- ◯ She throws him a rope.
- ◯ She uses a boat.
- ◯ She grabs his collar.
- ◯ She uses a ladder.

Test Tips

- Work step by step.
- Identify the important words in the questions.
- Refer to the story to answer the questions.

STOP

America's People

America is made up of many diverse people. Some were born in America. Others came from faraway countries. Discover some of these ordinary and extraordinary people and how they have helped to shape America.

Fine Art
Theme Connection

Look at the painting *New York: Statue of Liberty, 1886.*

- What do you see?
- Why do you think the Statue of Liberty is such an important symbol to Americans?

Read the article to find the meanings of these words, which are also in "April and Her Family":

✦ explorer
✦ orchid
✦ chores
✦ discovered
✦ sesame
✦ popular
✦ wiser

Vocabulary Strategy

Context Clues in the text help you find the meanings of words. Use context clues to find the meanings of *orchid, chores,* and *wiser*.

Vocabulary

Warm-Up

If you go to San Francisco, you should visit Chinatown. You will feel like an explorer in another country.

You can admire the beautiful flowers. You might even see an orchid or two.

You will pass by rows and rows of shops. The shops are filled with exotic toys.

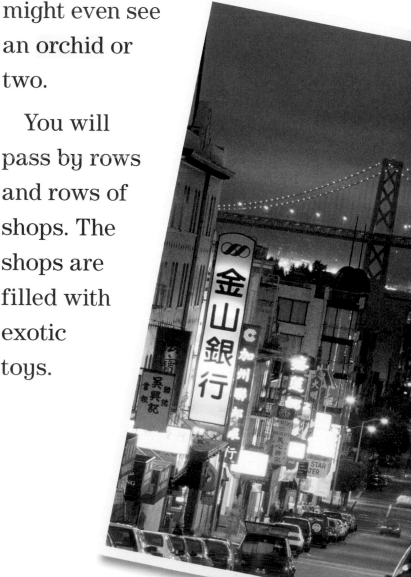

After the children who live in Chinatown have finished their chores, such as cleaning their rooms and washing the dishes, they play in front of the shops. You might even get to play with them!

You will be glad you discovered Chinatown when you smell the food. The aroma of food made with sesame oil drifts through the air.

There is even a playground in Chinatown. It is a popular place to visit. Children can run, climb, and play. Bright murals decorate the walls around the playground.

You will be wiser when you leave Chinatown because you will know more about a country that is really far away.

GAME

Sentence Building
Write a sentence for each of the selection vocabulary words. Draw a picture to go with one of your sentences.

Concept Vocabulary

The concept word for this lesson is *tradition.* A *tradition* is "a custom or belief that is passed on from generation to generation." What traditions does your family have?

April and Her Family

from

How My Family Lives in America

by Susan Kuklin

Focus Questions

Is everyone who lives in America alike? How do our differences make America stronger?

My name in America is April. I also have a Chinese name: *Chin* (ching), which means "admire" and *Lan* (lan), which means "orchid."

Both my parents are Chinese and were born in Taiwan. Taiwan is an island on the other side of the world. My papa came to New York without his parents to go to school and my mama moved here with her family. Because Julius, my older brother, and May, my older sister, and I were born in America, we are called Chinese Americans.

Orchid

Admire

There are many Chinese Americans. But we do not all speak the same Chinese language. The way my family speaks Chinese is called Mandarin.

In Mandarin, I call my daddy *baba* (bah–bah) and my mommy *mama* (mah–mah). It sounds something like English, but when we write the words they look very different. Another thing that's different in Chinese is that words aren't made with letters. Each word has its own special marks.

爸爸
Father

媽媽
Mother

During the week we go to public school, but on Saturday we go to Chinese school. There we learn how to speak and write in Chinese, like my parents learned in Taiwan. When I write English letters, I write from the left side of the page to the right. When I write in Chinese, I write from the right to the left. And I write in rows from the top of the page to the bottom. For us Chinese-American kids there are many things to remember.

In Chinese school we also learn a special kind of writing called calligraphy. We use a brush instead of a pen, black ink, and special paper made from stalks of rice. Our teacher shows us the right way to hold the brush.

My favorite part of Chinese school is snack time. Today, Mama made me cold sesame noodles, *tsu ma liang mein* (tsu mah leeang mee–en). I eat them with a fork, but most Chinese people eat their noodles with chopsticks. I'm just learning to eat with chopsticks.

Papa told us that an Italian explorer named Marco Polo discovered noodles in China a long time ago and introduced them to his country.

When Mama brought home takeout, Julius asked if a Chinese explorer discovered pizza in Italy.

Mama and Papa laughed and said, "No."

芝蔴涼麵

Cold Sesame Noodles

While we eat our pizza we play a game to test our wits. Papa asks us to look for letters hidden in the picture on the pizza box. Julius sees a *V* in the pizza man's shoe. May finds an *L*.

Oh, look! I can even see the Chinese letter *Ba* (bah), in the pizza man's eyebrows. *Ba* means "eight" in Chinese.

Eight

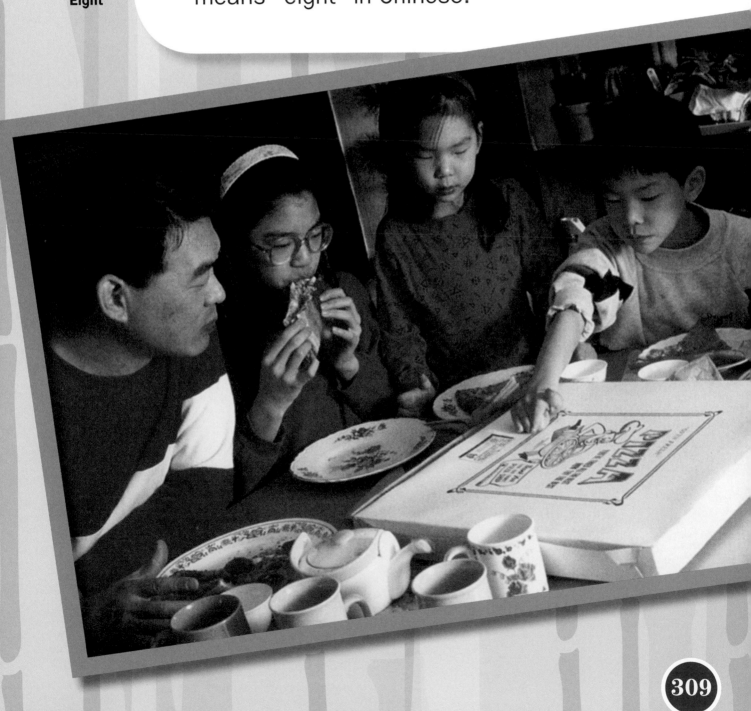

309

At night when we have finished all our chores and all our homework, we play *Chi chiao bang* (chee chow bang). In America some people call it Tangram. This is a popular game in Taiwan, like checkers is in America. My grandparents and even my great-grandparents played this game. To play, you move seven different shapes to build a new shape. I like to make a pussycat. It is very difficult, but I can do it. Papa says, "Go slowly and think about a cat. After a while your mind will start to run and you will see the cat in the shapes." He's right.

七
巧
板
Chi chiao bang

There is an old Chinese saying, "The older you are the wiser you become." When I become a grown-up, I will remember to tell this to my family.

Meet the Author

Susan Kuklin

Kuklin grew up in Philadelphia where her family introduced her to art, theater, and literature. She always wanted to be a ballerina or a stage actress and even went to acting school. She became a professional photographer later in her life. Her first children's book was about a chimpanzee named Nim who learned to communicate using sign language. Kuklin has taken photographs and written books for children about going to the doctor, fighting fires, and learning to dance.

America's People

Theme Connections

Within the Selection
1. Why did April's parents move to America?
2. What are some customs and traditions that April's parents are passing on to her?

Beyond the Selection
3. Where did your ancestors live?
4. Have you always lived in America?
5. Think about how "April and Her Family" adds to what you know about the theme America's People.

Write about It!
Describe a game you play with your family.

Remember to look for pictures and articles about America and its people to add to the **Concept/Question Board.**

313

Country Life, City Life

My grandparents live on a small farm. They raise cows and pigs. Every morning my grandfather goes outside to feed the animals. Then he milks the cows.

When I visit, we have strawberries and cream for breakfast. There is a big fireplace in the kitchen. There is a rocking chair too. Sometimes I sit and rock while Grandma cooks.

It is quiet at the farm. At night I sit on the porch swing with Grandma.

It is different at my house. We live in the city. It is very noisy! I hear trucks and traffic and barking dogs.

I am always rushing to get somewhere. I have soccer, school, and homework. I rush to do my chores. There is not much time to relax.

It is fun to live in the city, but I like the quiet time at my grandparents' too.

1. What word in the first sentence lets you know this story is a narrative?

2. Why might someone think visiting a farm is peaceful?

3. How is your daily life different from your ancestors' daily life?

Try It!

As you work on your investigation, present some of your facts in the form of a narrative story to make the information more interesting.

315

318 319

Read the article to find the meanings of these words, which are also in "New Hope":

✦ brisk
✦ doe
✦ leather
✦ shed
✦ recycling
✦ fabric
✦ citizens
✦ adopted

Vocabulary Strategy

Context Clues in the text help you find the meanings of words. Use context clues to find the meanings of *brisk* and *shed*.

Vocabulary

Warm-Up

As the ferry pulled into the port, the brisk wind blew. Mom wrapped up baby Emily to protect her from the cold.

This was our new home. But it did not feel like home. The plains stretched as far as the eye could see. A doe hid behind some trees.

Our first stop was Uncle Jeffrey's leather shop. Uncle Jeffrey is Dad's brother. He was glad to see us. He moved here two years ago.

We stayed with Uncle Jeffrey. After a few days of rest, we began to work. "We must begin to gather wood," Dad said. "Winter will be here soon."

That first winter was hard. Dad and I built a shed next to Uncle Jeffrey's house. We stored some of Uncle Jeffrey's things there to make room for us in his house.

We did not have much, and we did not waste anything. Mom reused boxes and jars. She said we were recycling.

In the spring, Dad began to work with Uncle Jeffrey. They sold fabric to the citizens of our town. Dad began to make money.

Soon there was enough money for me to quit working and go to school. I made many friends. That is when I began to love our adopted home.

Fill In the Blank
On a sheet of paper, use each of the vocabulary words in a sentence. Draw a blank line in place of each vocabulary word. Give your paper to another student. Have your partner fill in each blank with the correct vocabulary word.

Concept Vocabulary

The concept word for this lesson is **ancestors.** *Ancestors* are "people from whom a person or a group have descended." A grandfather and a great-grandmother are ancestors. Who are some of your ancestors?

NEW HOPE

by Henri Sorensen

Focus Questions

What does it mean to have hope? How do you think towns and communities first got started in our country?

Jimmy loved to visit Grandpa. He loved the old-fashioned ice-cream store in New Hope, where Grandpa lived. He loved the recycling dump. And he especially loved the statue in the park. "Who is that man?" Jimmy always asked. And every time, Grandpa told him the same wonderful story.

"That's Lars Jensen," Grandpa began. "Over one hundred years ago, in 1885, Lars sailed to this country from Denmark. He brought his wife, Karen, and their two children, Peter and Mathilde, to start a new life in America.

"When they landed in New York, they took a train to Minnesota. There Lars bought a wagon, two horses, a hunting rifle, tools, a tent, several bags of seeds, and plenty of food for the trip. Then he and Karen and Peter and Mathilde began the last part of their long journey. On narrow trails, they traveled through forests and forded rivers and crossed the wide plains.

"Sometimes they joined up with other travelers and Peter and Mathilde fell asleep to tales of Sitting Bull told around the campfire. One night a yellow dog appeared at the campsite. 'He must have followed us from the town we passed through this morning,' said Karen. 'Well, we can't take him back now,' said Lars. So Peter and Mathilde adopted him. They named him Fido.

"One day, just as they came to a river, one of the axles on their wagon broke. Lars took off his hat and scratched his head. Fish were jumping in the river. A doe and her fawn stood at the edge of the forest. *'Pokkers!'* said Lars. 'This looks like a good place. Let's stop here.'

"By the time the first snow fell, they had planted and harvested their first crop and built a small cabin for themselves and a shed for their horses. Each morning after checking their traps, Lars and Peter worked on the fence until Karen called them in for hot stew and bread.

"The following spring, while Karen and Mathilde worked in the garden, Lars and Peter built a small ferry. All that summer Lars ferried people and wagons across the river. Business was brisk—Lars's ferry was the only way to cross the river for miles.

"One day a blacksmith named Franz arrived. A busy ferry landing would bring lots of business, so instead of crossing the river, he stayed to build a forge.

"Soon lumbermen arrived to harvest the rich forests and farmers began to clear the land for their crops. 'All these people need a general store,' said Lars, so he traveled several days to the nearest big town to buy rope and shoes and nails and fabric and all the other things he knew the people would need. He named his shop the New Hope General Store.

"As the years passed, more and more people came to the village by the river. The old slow-moving ferry was replaced by a wooden bridge. Now that crossing the river was so easy, the stage coach began to stop at the New Hope General Store. One day a traveler named Saul got off the stage and stayed. Three months later he opened the New Hope Hotel.

"New Hope became a busy, bustling place. A wagon builder set up shop next door to the general store. Then came a bank and a stable and a barbershop and a newspaper office. The *New Hope Gazette* printed all the news and invitations and signs too. Soon Main Street had shops on both sides and a church with a bell in its steeple at the north end.

"In 1900, Mathilde married Franz's son Heinrich in that very church, and the whole town came to celebrate the wedding. Mathilde and Heinrich moved into a house on the brand-new street of Maple Lane, and Heinrich built the New Hope Tannery to make the best leather gloves and saddles and boots west of the Appalachian Mountains.

"By 1910, when Mathilde's little boy, Hans, was four years old, the railroad had come to New Hope. On it came traveling actors and salesmen and businessmen and friends and some people who stayed and became new citizens."

"And then what, Grandpa?" Jimmy asked.

"And then came me," said Grandpa. "Hans grew up to be my daddy and your great-grandpa."

"Tell about the statue," said Jimmy.

"When I was five years old," said Grandpa, "New Hope built this statue, and your great-grandpa told me the story that I just told you. It's a statue of Lars Jensen—your great-great-great-grandfather—who started this town because his axle broke."

333

Family History

My aunt has spent years collecting information about our family's history. I asked my aunt to help me learn more about our family. She found out that some of our family once lived in Italy. Others lived in France.

She handed me a birth certificate. The name on the certificate was Rose Scanga. The date was April 1, 1920.

"That was your grandma's mother," she said. "She was born in Italy. She came to America on a boat in 1940."

"Are we from Italy?" I asked.

"We are from France too," my aunt said.

"America is full of people from all places," I said to my aunt.

"That is what makes our country so great!" she exclaimed.

1. Which word in the first sentence lets you know this story is a narrative?

2. Where did the narrator's family come from?

3. Locate France, Italy, and the United States on the map.

Try It!

As you work on your investigation, think about how you can use a map to show your facts.

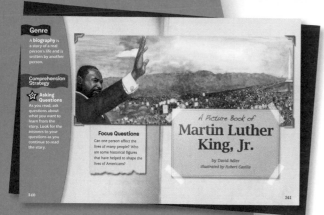

Read the article to find the meanings of these words, which are also in "A Picture Book of Martin Luther King, Jr.":

✦ demanding
✦ fair
✦ laws
✦ graduated
✦ arrested
✦ prejudice
✦ content
✦ section

Vocabulary Strategy

Use **apposition** to find the meanings of *graduated* and *section.*

Vocabulary

Warm-Up

Jonah's father was a powerful man. People listened to him when he talked. Jonah listened too. But sometimes he thought his father was too demanding. Jonah wanted to play. His father said, "Do your homework, and clean your room first."

Jonah thought it would be fair to do his homework before he played. But he wanted to clean his room after he came inside. Jonah tried to reason with his father.

"We have rules at home that are just like laws," said his father. "You must finish your homework and your chores before you play."

338

Jonah's father was a lawyer. He had graduated, or finished school, with honors. Jonah was proud of his father. Jonah knew his father helped people who had been arrested and helped to fight prejudice. Jonah thought about how other people felt about his father and the content of his character.

Jonah forgot he had been angry. Before he knew it, he had finished his homework and had begun to clean his room. He organized his closet and cleaned every section, or part, of his room. As Jonah was putting the last book on his shelf, he had an idea. "Dad," he said, "I think I want to be a lawyer just like you!"

"You will be a good one," smiled his father.

GAME

Fill In the Blank
On a sheet of paper, use each of the selection vocabulary words in a sentence. Draw a blank line in place of each vocabulary word. Give your paper to another student. Have your partner fill in each blank with the correct vocabulary word.

Concept Vocabulary

The concept word for this lesson is *value.* *Value* means "to think highly of." People value different things. Talk about different things that people value. What things did Jonah's father value?

Genre

A **biography** is a story of a real person's life and is written by another person.

Comprehension Strategy

 Asking Questions

As you read, ask questions about what you want to learn from the story. Look for the answers to your questions as you continue to read the story.

Focus Questions

Can one person affect the lives of many people? Who are some historical figures that have helped to shape the lives of Americans?

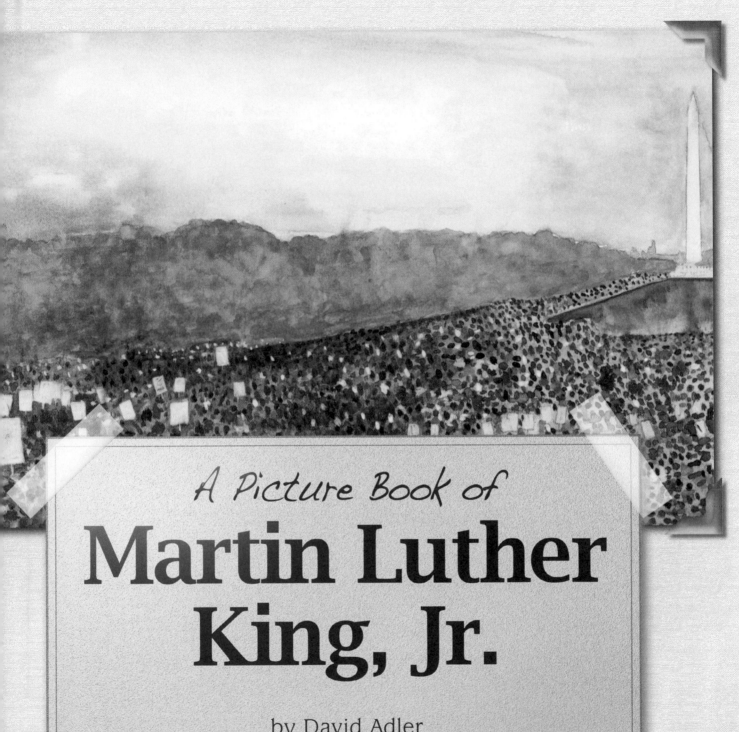

A Picture Book of
Martin Luther King, Jr.

by David Adler

illustrated by Robert Casilla

Martin Luther King, Jr. was one of America's great leaders. He was a powerful speaker, and he spoke out against laws which kept black people out of many schools and jobs. He led protests and marches demanding fair laws for all people.

Martin Luther King, Jr. was born on January 15, 1929 in Atlanta, Georgia. Martin's father was a pastor. His mother had been a teacher. Martin had an older sister, Willie Christine, and a younger brother, Alfred Daniel.

Young Martin liked to play baseball, football and basketball. He liked to ride his bicycle and to sing. He often sang in his father's church.

Martin (center) with his brother Alfred Daniel (left) and his sister Willie Christine (right)

Young Martin played in his backyard with his friends. One day he was told that two of his friends would no longer play with him, because they were white and he was black.

Martin cried. He didn't understand why the color of his skin should matter to anyone.

Martin's mother told him that many years ago black people were brought in chains to America and sold as slaves. She told him that long before Martin was born the slaves had been set free. However, there were still some people who did not treat black people fairly.

In Atlanta, where Martin lived, and elsewhere in the United States, there were "White Only" signs. Black people were not allowed in some parks, pools, hotels, restaurants and even schools. Blacks were kept out of many jobs.

Martin learned to read at home before he was old enough to start school. All through his childhood, he read books about black leaders.

Harriet Tubman

Frederick Douglass

George Washington Carver

Martin was a good student. He finished high school two years early and was just fifteen when he entered Morehouse College in Atlanta. At college Martin decided to become a minister.

After Martin was graduated from Morehouse, he studied for a doctorate at Boston University. While he was there he met Coretta Scott. She was studying music. They fell in love and married.

In 1954 Martin Luther King, Jr. began his first job as a pastor in Montgomery, Alabama. The next year Rosa Parks, a black woman, was arrested in Montgomery. She had been sitting just behind the "White Only" section on the bus. When all the seats in that section were taken, the driver told her to get up so a white man could have her seat. Rosa Parks refused.

Dr. Martin Luther King, Jr. led a protest.
Blacks throughout the city refused to ride the
buses. Dr. King said, "There comes a time
when people get tired of being kicked about."

One night, while Dr. King was at a meeting, someone threw a bomb into his house.

Martin's followers were angry. They wanted to fight. Martin told them to go home peacefully. "We must love our white brothers," he said. "We must meet hate with love."

The bus protest lasted almost a year. When it ended there were no more "White Only" sections on buses.

Dr. King decided to move back to Atlanta in 1960. There, he continued to lead peaceful protests against "White Only" waiting rooms, lunch counters and rest rooms. He led many marches for freedom.

In 1963 Dr. King led the biggest march of all—the March on Washington. More than two hundred thousand black and white people followed him. "I have a dream," he said in his speech. "I have a dream that my four children will one day live in a nation where they will not be judged by the color of their skin but by the content of their character."

The next year in 1964, Dr. King was awarded one of the greatest honors any person can win, the Nobel Peace Prize.

The country was changing. New laws were passed. Blacks could go to the same schools as whites. They could go to the same stores, restaurants and hotels. "White Only" signs were against the law.

Dr. King told his followers to protest peacefully. But there were some riots and some violence.

Then, in April 1968, Dr. King went to Memphis, Tennessee. He planned to march so black and white garbage workers would get the same pay for the same work.

On April 4 in Memphis, Dr. King stood outside his motel room. Another man, James Earl Ray, was hiding nearby. He pointed a rifle at Dr. King. He fired the gun. An hour later Dr. King was dead.

Martin Luther King, Jr. dreamed of a world free of hate, prejudice and violence. Carved on the stone which marks his grave are the words, "I'm free at last."

Meet the Author

David Adler

As a child, Adler was known for his artistic ability, and he would often tell stories to his brothers and sisters.

Adler was a math teacher, a cartoonist, and an arts and crafts teacher before he became a writer. He wrote his first children's book while he was a math teacher. He gets many ideas for his stories by watching and listening to other people.

Meet the Illustrator

Robert Casilla

Casilla said, "I find great rewards and satisfaction in illustrating for children."

He has illustrated ten other biographies written by David Adler. When he illustrates a biography, he first tries to learn a lot about the person. Knowing the person very well helps him when he works on the art.

America's People

Theme Connections

Within the Selection

1. How did Martin Luther King Jr. make a difference in people's lives?

2. Why was Martin Luther King Jr. willing to put himself in danger to help others?

Across Selections

3. How was Peter in "The Hole in the Dike" similar to Martin Luther King Jr.?

Beyond the Selection

4. Think about how "A Picture Book of Martin Luther King, Jr." adds to what you know about America's People.

Write about It!

Do you think Martin Luther King Jr.'s actions still affect Americans today? How?

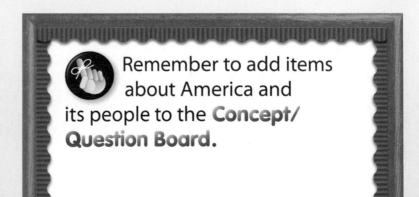

Remember to add items about America and its people to the Concept/Question Board.

George Washington

George Washington was born in 1732. He was the first president of the United States of America.

IN THE ARMY

Washington was a good student. But he went to school for only seven or eight years. Then he joined the army. Soon Washington became the leader of the army.

America was fighting to be a free country. After many years, Washington and the army won the war.

THE FIRST PRESIDENT

People believed George Washington was fair. They made him the first president in 1789. Washington was president for eight years.

PRESIDENTS' DAY

The third Monday in February is called Presidents' Day. This is a national holiday when we honor George Washington and another president, Abraham Lincoln.

Genre

Expository Text is written to inform or explain. It contains facts about real people, things, or events.

Feature

Headings tell what a paragraph is going to be about.

1. How are the headings helpful?

2. When is Presidents' Day?

3. Do you think Washington was a good soldier in the army? Why or why not?

Try It!

As you work on your investigation, think about how you could use headings to organize your information.

Read the article to find the meanings of these words, which are also in "Jingle Dancer":

- ✦ calves
- ✦ ached
- ✦ pounding
- ✦ pale
- ✦ glimpse
- ✦ shuffled
- ✦ slipped
- ✦ strolled

Vocabulary Strategy

Use **word structure** to determine the meanings of *ached, shuffled, slipped,* and *strolled.*

Vocabulary
Warm-Up

Rosie's calves ached. She had a pounding headache. She was sweaty and pale. "Only a mile to go," she thought. "I have practiced running every day to get ready for this race. I can do this."

Rosie sprinted on. While she ran, she thought about her grandmother. Rosie remembered the photos she had seen. "The photos give me only a glimpse of

Grandma's life," she thought. "I wish I had known Grandma when she was a track star."

The end of the race was just ahead. Rosie's thoughts turned to daydreams. She pictured a younger version of her grandma. She saw her jumping hurdles. She saw her doing relays. Rosie saw her grandma as she had never seen her before. "Dad was right. I have running in my blood just like Grandma," thought Rosie.

Rosie shuffled across the finish line. She came in tenth place. Rosie slipped on a cool jacket and strolled to her car. A smile tugged at the corner of Rosie's mouth. She was still thinking of her grandmother.

GAME

Charades
Use the vocabulary words to play a game of charades with your classmates. Choose one of the words to act out. The first person to correctly identify the word and explain its meaning gets to take the next turn.

Concept Vocabulary

The concept word for this lesson is *legacy.* A *legacy* is "something that is passed down from generation to generation." Why is leaving a legacy important?

Genre

Realistic Fiction is a story that did not happen, but the characters, places, and events in the story seem real.

Comprehension Strategy

⭐ **Adjusting Reading Speed** As you read, check to make sure you understand what you are reading and slow down or speed up your reading accordingly.

Jingle Dancer

by Cynthia Leitich Smith

illustrated by Cornelius Van Wright and Ying-Hwa Hu

Focus Questions

Why do people practice traditions? What does it mean to keep a cultural tradition "alive"?

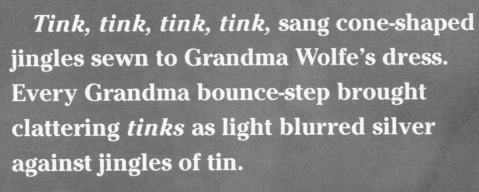

Tink, tink, tink, tink, sang cone-shaped jingles sewn to Grandma Wolfe's dress. Every Grandma bounce-step brought clattering *tinks* as light blurred silver against jingles of tin.

Jenna daydreamed at the kitchen table, tasting honey on fry bread, her heart beating to the *brum, brum, brum, brum* of the powwow drum.

As Moon kissed Sun good night, Jenna shifted her head on Grandma Wolfe's shoulder. "I want to jingle dance, too."

"Next powwow, you could dance Girls," Grandma Wolfe answered. "But we don't have enough time to mail-order tins for rolling jingles."

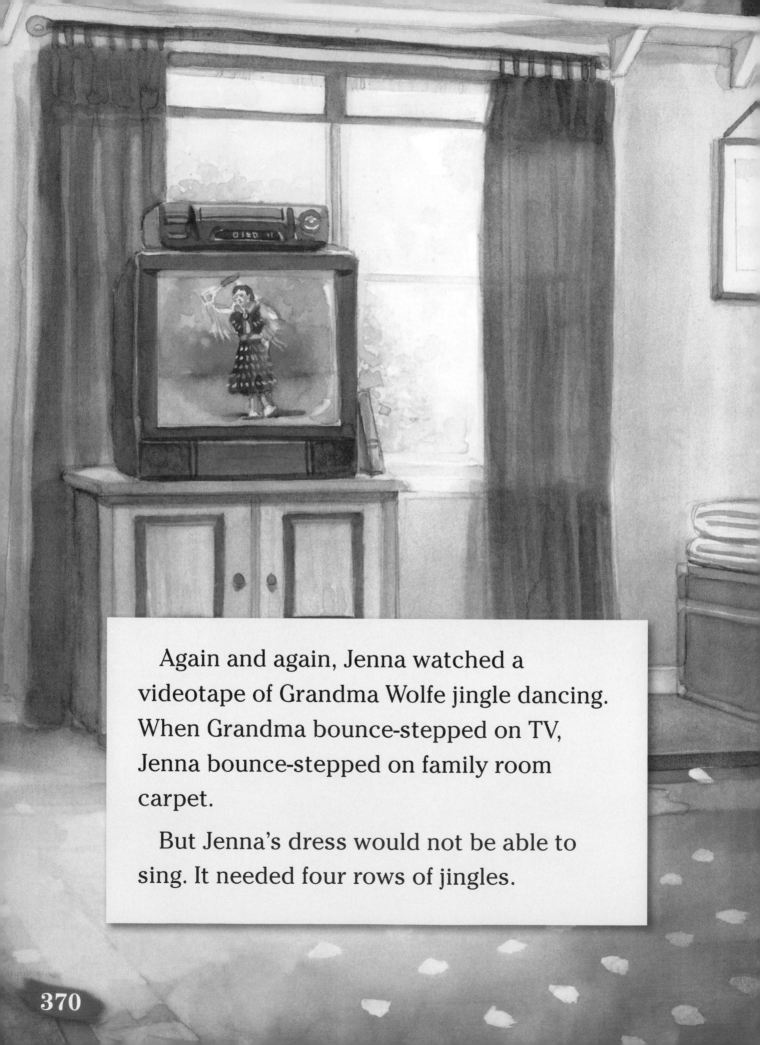

Again and again, Jenna watched a videotape of Grandma Wolfe jingle dancing. When Grandma bounce-stepped on TV, Jenna bounce-stepped on family room carpet.

But Jenna's dress would not be able to sing. It needed four rows of jingles.

As Sun fetched morning, Jenna danced east to Great-aunt Sis's porch. Jenna's bounce-steps crunched autumn leaves, but her steps didn't jingle.

373

Once again, Great-aunt Sis told Jenna a Muscogee Creek story about Bat. Although other animals had said he was too small to make a difference, Bat won a ball game by flying high and catching a ball in his teeth.

Rising sunlight reached through a windowpane and flashed against . . . what was it, hanging in Aunt Sis's bedroom?

Jingles on a dress too long quiet.

"May I borrow enough jingles to make a row?" Jenna asked, not wanting to take so many that Aunt Sis's dress would lose its voice.

"You may," Aunt Sis answered, rubbing her calves. "My legs don't work so good anymore. Will you dance for me?"

"I will," said Jenna with a kiss on Aunt Sis's cheek.

Now Jenna's dress needed three more rows.

375

As Sun arrived at midcircle, Jenna skipped south to Mrs. Scott's brand-new duplex. At Jenna's side, jingles clinked.

Mrs. Scott led Jenna into the kitchen. Once again, Jenna rolled dough, and Mrs. Scott fried it.

"May I borrow enough jingles to make a row?" Jenna asked, not wanting to take so many that Mrs. Scott's dress would lose its voice.

"You may," Mrs. Scott answered, tossing flour with her apron. "At powwow, I'll be busy selling fry bread and Indian tacos. Will you dance for me?"

"I will," said Jenna with a high five.

Now Jenna's dress needed two more rows.

As Sun caught a glimpse of Moon, Jenna strolled west to Cousin Elizabeth's apartment. At Jenna's side, jingles clanked.

Elizabeth had arrived home late from the law firm. Once again, Jenna helped Elizabeth carry in her files.

"May I borrow enough jingles to make a row?" Jenna asked, not wanting to take so many that Elizabeth's dress would lose its voice.

"You may," Elizabeth answered, burrowing through her messy closet for her jingle dress. "This weekend, I'm working on a big case and can't go to powwow. Will you dance for me?"

"I will," said Jenna, clasping her cousin's hands.

Now Jenna's dress needed one more row of jingles, but she didn't know which way to turn.

As Moon glowed pale, Jenna shuffled north to Grandma Wolfe's. At Jenna's side, jingles sat silent. High above, clouds wavered like worried ghosts.

When Jenna tugged open the door, jingles sang, *tink, tink, tink, tink*. Grandma Wolfe was jingle dancing on TV. Jenna breathed in every *hey-ah-ho-o* of a powwow song. Her heart beat *brum, brum, brum, brum* to the pounding of the drum.

On family room carpet, beaded moccasins waited for Jenna's feet. She shucked off a sneaker and slipped on a moccasin that long before had danced with Grandma Wolfe.

Jenna knew where to find her fourth row.

"May I borrow enough jingles to make a row?" Jenna asked, not wanting to take so many that Grandma Wolfe's dress would lose its voice.

"You may," Grandma said with a hug.

Now Jenna's dress could sing.

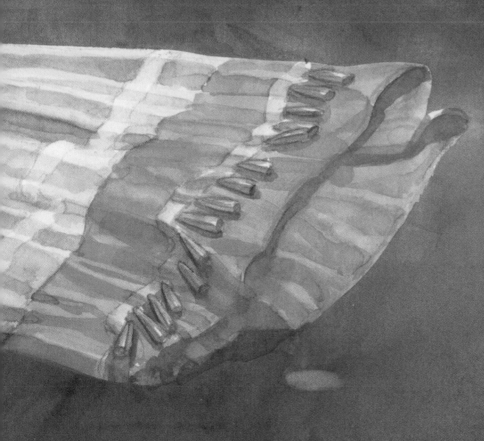

Every night that week, Jenna helped Grandma Wolfe sew on jingles and bring together the dance regalia.

Every night, Jenna practiced her bounce-steps.

Brum, brum, brum, brum, sounded the drum at the powwow the next weekend. As light blurred silver, Jenna jingle danced . . . for Great-aunt Sis, whose legs ached,

. . . for Mrs. Scott, who sold fry bread,

. . . for Elizabeth, who worked on her big case,

. . . and for Grandma Wolfe, who warmed
like Sun. *Tink, tink, tink, tink.*

Meet the Author

Cynthia Leitich Smith

Smith is a tribal member of the Muscogee (Creek) Nation of Native Americans. She has had many different jobs, including a gas station attendant and an English tutor for migrant workers. She now writes children's books and teaches writing to college students.

Meet the Illustrators

Cornelius Van Wright and Ying-Hwa Hu

Van Wright and Hu are a husband and wife illustration team who have worked together on several projects. They work so closely together that they say it is sometimes difficult for them to tell their art apart.

America's People

Theme Connections

Within the Selection

1. Why do you think Jenna wanted to jingle dance?

2. Do you think Jenna enjoyed dancing at the powwow? Why or why not?

Across Selections

3. How is Jenna like April in "April and Her Family"? How is she different?

Beyond the Selection

4. What could you do that would tell others about your culture?

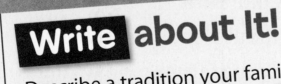

Write about It!

Describe a tradition your family has.

Remember to look for items about America and its people to add to the **Concept/Question Board.**

Genre

Newspaper Articles tell about people, places, or things that happen in nations, states, and cities.

Feature

Quotations are statements made by people in an article or a story.

Local Resident Traces Roots

by Mike Bell

Tara Plink is excited. She just learned that she has a famous relative. "My great-grandfather was Tom Plink," says Tara. "He was a famous author. He wrote thirteen books."

How did Tara learn about her great-grandfather? "I talked to a lot of people. I asked them questions," Tara says. "I looked at birth certificates and old newspaper articles. I looked at photos too!"

Tara wanted to trace her family tree. "It helps me know who I am. It helps me know where I came from. I also get to see a glimpse of the past," she explains.

Tara is going to lead a workshop. It will be held at the high school. Tara has worked hard to find her roots. She wants to help other people do the same. "It takes time to trace your family history," says Tara. "But it is fun to know about your family."

1. How do you know when Tara is talking?

2. Why might someone consider tracing his or her roots?

3. What are some ways you could find out more about past generations of your family?

Try It!

As you work on your investigation, remember to look in newspaper articles for facts and information.

Read the article to find the meanings of these words, which are also in "Cesar E. Chavez":

- ✦ treated
- ✦ border
- ✦ weakened
- ✦ strike
- ✦ union
- ✦ boycott
- ✦ crops
- ✦ awarded

Vocabulary Strategy

Use **apposition** to find the meanings of *border* and *awarded*.

Vocabulary

Warm-Up

Throughout history there have been many brave people. Some brave people are famous. Others just worked hard to do what was right. My grandpa worked hard. He treated others fairly.

My grandpa was a cotton farmer in Texas. Grandpa hired workers from over the border, or line, in Mexico. He paid them a good wage to help him pick cotton.

His neighbors were not as fair. Grandpa's neighbors made the people who picked their cotton work long hours. The days were long. The sun was hot. The cotton pickers were weakened.

Grandpa got mad. He talked to the people who picked cotton. He told them he would understand if they wanted to strike. He told them how he was once in a union. Grandpa's union helped keep him safe when he was a coal miner. Grandpa told the workers they should form a union.

Some people got mad at my grandpa. He did not care. He always said, "Fair is fair, and right is right." Grandpa joined a cotton boycott. He lost money on his cotton that year. But he had other crops.

Grandpa should have been awarded, or given, a prize. He stood for all the right things.

GAME

Matching Game
Write each vocabulary word on an index card. Then write each word's meaning on its own card. Turn over and spread out the cards. Take turns with a partner matching each word with its meaning.

Concept Vocabulary

The concept word for this lesson is **equality.** *Equality* means "to have equal rights." Can you think of people who have worked hard for equality? Why is equality important?

Genre

A **biography** is a story of a real person's life and is written by another person.

Comprehension Skill

 Drawing Conclusions

As you read, use the information in the text to draw conclusions about the characters or the events in the story.

CESAR E. CHAVEZ

by Don McLeese

Focus Questions

Why is it important for all people to be treated fairly? Can one person's actions affect an entire country?

STRIKE

EQUALITY NOW!

Cesar and farm workers

THE FARM WORKER'S HERO

Cesar E. Chavez is a hero to **Mexican Americans** and to everyone who believes that workers should be treated fairly. He brought farm workers together into a **union.** Led by Chavez, they said they wouldn't pick grapes unless they were paid and treated better. **Grape pickers** have a better life today because of Chavez.

FROM MEXICO TO THE UNITED STATES

Cesar was named for his grandfather, Cesario Chavez. Cesario was born and lived in Mexico. He worked hard on a Mexican ranch but was very poor. In the 1880s he crossed the border into Texas, looking for a better life. He moved his whole family to Arizona, where they worked on the farms.

Cesar and his family worked the fields.

Cesar with his brother, Manuel, and his mother, Juana

CESAR'S FAMILY

Cesar Estrada Chavez was born March 31, 1927, near Yuma, Arizona. His father was Librado Chavez, Cesario's son. His mother was named Juana. She had also moved from Mexico. Cesar was their second child and first son. Librado was a hard worker. He opened a store as well as working on the farm.

CESAR'S SCHOOLS

The family moved around so much that Cesar once guessed that he had gone to 65 different grade schools! His family still spoke Spanish at home, as his grandfather had in Mexico. In school, they spoke only English, which made learning harder for Cesar. He quit school after the eighth grade to work in the fields.

Cesar's eighth grade graduation photo

Cesar lived in California after the Great Depression.

MOVING TO CALIFORNIA

The 1930s were a very bad time in the United States. This time was called the **Great Depression,** because many people were so poor. Few people had much money and many had no jobs. In 1938 the Chavez family lost its farm and moved to California. There they picked **crops** for other farms.

WORKING THE FIELDS

During World War II, Cesar joined the Navy. When he returned from the war in 1946, he continued to pick crops in California. In 1948 he married Helen Fabela. They had eight children. It was hard to support a family with farm work, and he began to fight for change.

UNITED FARM WORKERS

Through the 1950s and 1960s, Cesar worked with unions to make life better in the field. In 1965, he asked grape pickers to **strike,** or to refuse to work. He asked all Americans to **boycott,** or quit buying, grapes. Over the next decade, Cesar became a worker's hero as the leader of the **United Farm Workers.**

Cesar and the United Farm Workers banner

HUNGER STRIKES

Cesar had twice gone on hunger strikes, refusing to eat, and these may have weakened him. He spent his last days in Arizona, near where he was born. Throughout the Mexican-American community, he is as important as Dr. Martin Luther King, Jr., is for civil rights.

After ending his hunger strike, Cesar sat with Robert F. Kennedy.

Cesar E. Chavez

CESAR LIVES!

Cesar E. Chavez died on April 23, 1993, but his memory lives on. California celebrates March 31 as Cesar Chavez Day, making his birthday a state holiday.

In 1994, after his death, President Bill Clinton awarded him the U.S. Medal of Freedom. Every farm worker who enjoys a better life owes thanks to Cesar E. Chavez.

Meet the Author

Don McLeese

McLeese first began to write children's books when his two daughters were young. Until that time, he had mainly written for adults, but he discovered he really liked writing for children. He has written many biographies about famous people, including Native Americans, inventors, and heroes of the American Revolution. He now teaches college journalism classes, writes articles for magazines and newspapers, and writes books.

America's People

Theme Connections

Within the Selection

1. How did Chavez make a difference in people's lives?

2. Why do you think Chavez wanted to help farm workers?

Across Selections

3. Chavez is considered a hero to farm workers. What other heroes have you read about?

Beyond the Selection

4. Do you think Chavez's actions still affect people today? How?

Write about It!

Write about what you think it would be like to go on a hunger strike.

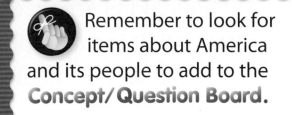

Remember to look for items about America and its people to add to the **Concept/Question Board.**

Science Inquiry

Pumpkins

Pumpkins are very easy to grow. Pumpkins love sunny spots. They can be planted in late spring or early summer.

The seeds need water. With *water* and *sunlight*, vines will soon cover the ground.

The first thing that grows on a pumpkin plant is three leaves. A pumpkin plant will grow quickly after these three leaves grow.

Ten weeks after a seed is planted, flowers appear. Pumpkin plants have two kinds of flowers—a *male* and a *female*. Bees gather pollen from the male flower and place it in the female flower.

Pumpkins are ready to harvest in the fall. It is fun to plant a small seed and end up with a huge pumpkin!

Think Link

1. How is the italic text helpful?

2. What are two kinds of flowers on a pumpkin plant?

3. Why might someone consider planting a pumpkin seed?

Try It!

As you work on your unit investigation, remember to use italic text to emphasize words.

421

Focus Questions

Who do you think were the first Americans?
Are immigrants still coming to America today?

America's People

from **America Is...**

by Louise Borden • *illustrated by Stacey Schuett*

America is home to its very first people:

    the proud tribes

    who live in peace

    with the earth

    and the sky,

    whose words bring wisdom

    to all who listen.

And America is those who came later:

    many kinds of people

    from many countries of the world.

    We are one family,

    and one team.

We are **Americans**.

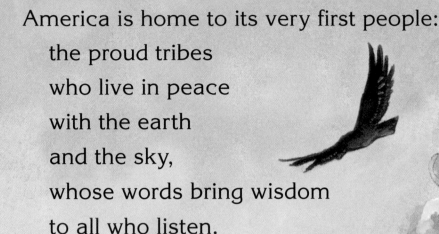

A poem is carved into the
base of the Statue of Liberty. What do you think
it should say to greet new immigrants? Why
do you think the Statue of Liberty is such an
important symbol to Americans?

STATUE OF LIBERTY

by Myra Cohn Livingston

Give me your tired, your poor, she says,
Those yearning to be free.
Take a light from my burning torch,
The light of Liberty.

Give me your huddled masses
Lost on another shore,
Tempest-tossed and weary,
These I will take and more.

Give me your thirsty, your hungry
Who come from another place.
You who would dream of freedom
Look into my face.

Test-Taking Strategy: Taking the Best Guess When Unsure of the Answer

Most of the time, you will know the answers on a test. Sometimes you might not. When this happens, take your best guess.

Taking the Best Guess When Unsure of the Answer

Try not to guess the answer too often. It is better to think about the question, look at the answer choices, and choose the one that you think is correct.

EXAMPLE
Read the sentence. Think about the answer that fits best in the blank.

1. The _____ flapped its wings and flew away.
○ salmon
○ caterpillar
○ pigeon

If you did not know that the correct answer is *pigeon*, you should have guessed. When you guess, you will be correct some of the time.

My Neighbors

My grandmother says we live in the best place in the world. When I ask her why, she says, "It is because of the people."

The store I like best is Luca's. It is the food market near our house. Mrs. Luca always has good fruit. She also sells wonderful bread. Mr. Luca is the baker. He makes fresh Italian bread every day. Their store always smells good.

When we are sick, we go to Dr. Hill. Her family came from Africa hundreds of years ago. Dr. Hill says her family is happy she is a doctor. I think she is the best doctor ever.

GO ON

My family likes to ride bikes. We all have bikes. Sometimes a bike needs to be fixed. We take it to Pedro's Bike Shop. He can fix anything on a bike. Pedro's family came to Florida from Cuba.

Mr. O'Hare helps us cross the street on our way to school. He says his ancestors are from Ireland. He always tells funny stories about his grandmother and grandfather. I love hearing his funny stories.

Now I understand what my grandmother means. The people do make this the best place in the world.

1. Grandmother likes where she lives because of _____.
   ○ the weather
   ○ the food
   ○ the people
   ○ the stores

2. What is Mr. Luca's job?
   ○ He is a baker.
   ○ He is a teacher.
   ○ He is a doctor.
   ○ He fixes bikes.

3. What does the family like to do?
   ○ Play golf
   ○ Ride bikes
   ○ Go fishing
   ○ Tell funny stories

4. This story is mostly about _____.
   ○ people and their jobs
   ○ telling funny stories
   ○ Dr. Hill's family
   ○ riding bikes

5. Who tells funny stories about his family?
   ○ Mr. Luca
   ○ Pedro
   ○ Mr. O'Hare
   ○ Dr. Hill

Test Tips

• Compare all the answer choices before choosing the one that best answers the question.

• If you do not know the answer, take your best guess.

STOP

Pronunciation Key

a as in **a**t
ā as in l**a**te
â as in c**a**re
ä as in f**a**ther
e as in s**e**t
ē as in m**e**
i as in **i**t
ī as in k**i**te
o as in **o**x
ō as in r**o**se

ô as in b**ou**ght and r**a**w
oi as in c**oi**n
o͞o as in b**oo**k
o͞o as in t**oo**
or as in f**or**m
ou as in **ou**t
u as in **u**p
ū as in **u**se
ûr as in t**ur**n, g**er**m, l**ear**n, f**ir**m, w**or**k

ə as in **a**bout, chick**e**n, penc**i**l, cann**o**n, circ**u**s
ch as in **ch**air
hw as in **wh**ich
ng as in ri**ng**
sh as in **sh**op
th as in **th**in
th̷ as in **th**ere
zh as in trea**s**ure

The mark (ˊ) is placed after a syllable with a heavy accent, as in **chicken** (chikˊ ən).

The mark (ˊ) after a syllable shows a lighter accent, as in **disappear** (disˊ ə pērˊ).

Glossary

A

ached (ākt) *v.* Past tense of **ache:** to hurt with a dull, steady pain.

admire (əd mīr´) *v.* To think well of someone or something.

adopted (ə dop təd´) *v.* To take as one's own.

afraid (ə frād´) *adj.* Feeling fear.

anemone (ə nem´ ə nē) *n.* A plant that has delicate white, red, pink, or purple flowers.

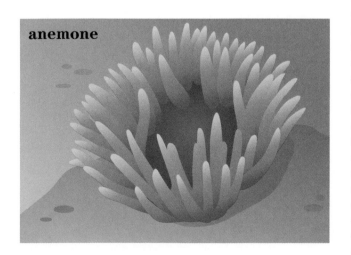
anemone

arrested (ə res´ təd) *v.* Past tense of **arrest:** to hold by authority of the law.

ashamed (ə shāmd´) *adj.* Feeling guilt.

available (ə vā´ lə bəl) *adj.* Being in the area and ready to use.

avalanche (av´ ə lanch´) *n.* Stones or snow rolling down a mountain.

avoid (ə void´) *v.* To stay away from someone or something.

awarded (ə wôr´ dəd) *v.* Past tense of **award:** to give a prize.

axles (ak´ səlz) *n.* Plural of **axle:** a rod on which the wheels of a wagon turn.

431

Pronunciation Key: a**t**; l**ā**te; c**â**re; f**ä**ther; s**e**t; m**ē**; **i**t; k**ī**te; **o**x; r**ō**se; **ô** in b**o**ught; c**oi**n; b**oo**k; t**oo**; f**o**rm; **ou**t; **u**p; **ū**se; t**û**rn; **ə** sound in **a**bout, chick**e**n, penc**i**l, cann**o**n, circ**u**s; **ch**air; **hw** in **wh**ich; ri**ng**; **sh**op; **th**in; **th**ere; **zh** in trea**s**ure

B

bank (bangk) *n.* The land along a stream.

barely (bâr´ lē) *adv.* Not very much.

barnacles (bär´ nə kəlz) *n.* Plural of **barnacle:** a small sea animal that has a shell and attaches itself to a rock, ship bottom, or another object in the water.

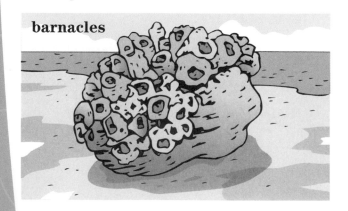

barnacles

blacksmith (blak´ smith´) *n.* A person who makes things out of iron.

blade (blād) *n.* A thin leaf.

blade

blend (blend) *v.* To mix together so as not to be seen.

blizzard (bliz´ ərd) *n.* A heavy snowstorm with very strong winds.

blocking (blok´ ing) *v.* In the way of something.

blossom (blos´ əm) *v.* To bloom.

blurred (blûrd) *v.* Past tense of **blur:** to become hard to see.

border (bôr´ dər) *n.* A line where one country or other area ends and another begins.

boycott (boi´ kot) *v.* To refuse to buy something until workers are treated better.

brave (brāv) *adj.* Not afraid.

brisk (brisk) *adj.* Quick and lively.

brook (brŏŏk) *n.* A small body of flowing water.

brook

burrowed (bûr´ ōd) *v.* Past tense of **burrow:** to dig.

burrowing (bûr´ ō ing) *v.* Digging.

bustling (bus´ ling) *adj.* Filled with activity.

C

calligraphy (ka´ lə gra´ fē) *n.* A special kind of handwriting.

calves (kavz) *n.* Plural of **calf:** the back part of the lower leg.

camouflage (kam´ ə fläzh) *n.* A disguise that makes something look the same as the area around it.

cattails (kat´ tālz´) *n.* Plural of **cattail:** a tall plant with a fuzzy brown top that grows in very wet areas.

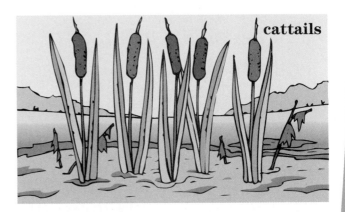

cattails

cautiously (kô´ shəs lē) *adv.* With care.

Pronunciation Key: at; lāte; câre; fäther; set; mē; it; kīte; ox; rōse; ô in bought; coin; book; too; form; out; up; ūse; tûrn; ə sound in about, chicken, pencil, cannon, circus; chair; hw in which; ring; shop; thin; there; zh in treasure

chopsticks (chop´ stiks) *n.* A pair of long, thin sticks used to eat with.

chores (chôrz) *n.* Plural of **chore**: a small job around the house.

citizens (sit´ i zenz) *n.* Plural of **citizen**: a person who was born in a country or who chooses to live in and become a member of a country.

coloration (kə´ lə rā´ shən) *n.* The way something is colored.

content (kən´ tent) *n.* What is in something.

continued (kən tin´ ūd) *v.* Past tense of **continue**: to keep doing.

costume (kos´ toom´) *n.* Something one wears to look like something else.

cottage (kot´ ij) *n.* A small house.

courage (kûr´ ij) *n.* The strength to overcome fear.

craned (krānd) *v.* Past tense of **crane**: to stretch out the neck in order to see better.

creatures (krē´ chərz) *n.* Plural of **creature**: a living thing.

crops (krops) *n.* Plural of **crop**: fruits, vegetables, or other plants that are grown on a farm and sold.

crops

crossed (crôsd) *v.* Past tense of **cross:** to move from one side of something to the other.

dash (dash) *n.* A short race.

decade (dek´ ād) *n.* Ten years.

delay (di lā´) *v.* To take place at a later time.

delicate (del´ i kit) *adj.* Not strong.

demanding (di mand´ ing) *v.* Asking for forcefully.

depends (di pendz´) *v.* Counts on someone.

designed (di zīnd´) *v.* Past tense of **design:** to plan or make.

dikes (dīks) *n.* Plural of **dike:** a thick wall built to hold back water.

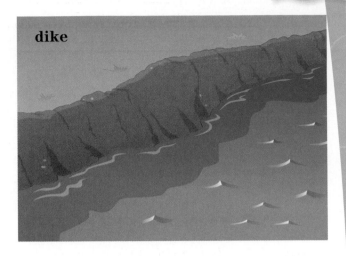

dike

dines (dīnz) *v.* Eats.

discovered (dis kəv´ ûrd) *v.* Past tense of **discover:** to be the first to find, learn of, or observe.

disguise (dis gīz´) *n.* Something that hides the way one looks.

doctorate (dok´ tər it) *n.* An award for graduating from the highest level of college.

doe (dō) *n.* A female deer.

doe

Pronunciation Key: at; l**ā**te; c**â**re; f**ä**ther; s**e**t; m**ē**; **i**t; k**ī**te; **o**x; r**ō**se; **ô** in b**ou**ght; c**oi**n; b**oo**k; t**oo**; f**or**m; **ou**t; **u**p; **ū**se; t**û**rn; **ə** sound in **a**bout, chick**e**n, penc**i**l, cann**o**n, circ**u**s; **ch**air; **hw** in **wh**ich; ri**ng**; **sh**op; **th**in; **th**ere; **zh** in trea**s**ure

drab (drab) *adj.* Plain and without color.

dragons (drag´ ənz) *n.* Plural of **dragon:** an imaginary beast that is supposed to look like a giant lizard with claws and wings.

dreaded (dre´ dəd) *v.* Past tense of **dread:** to be afraid of or anxious about something.

drift (drift) *v.* To move or pile up because of the movement of air or water.

drowsy (drou´ zē) *adj.* Feeling sleepy.

dump (dump) *n.* A place for garbage.

duplex (doo´ pleks) *n.* A house divided into two living units.

east (ēst) *adv.* A direction.

echo (ek´ ō) *n.* A repeated sound.

emperor (em´ pə rûr) *n.* A ruler.

enemies (en´ ə mēz) *n.* Plural of **enemy:** something or someone that is dangerous.

exclaimed (iks klāmd´) *v.* Past tense of **exclaim:** to cry out suddenly.

explorer (ek splôr´ ûr) *n.* A person who travels to a new place for the purpose of discovery.

F

fabric (fab´ rik) *n.* Cloth.

fade (fād) *v.* To lose color or brightness.

fail (fāl) *v.* To not succeed.

fair (fâr) *adj.* Not favoring one more than another.

fairly (fâr´ lē) *adv.* In a way that one is not favored more than another.

fawn (fôn) *n.* A young deer.

ferry (fâr´ ē) *n.* A boat used to carry people, cars, and goods across a narrow body of water.

ferry

fetched (fechd) *v.* Past tense of **fetch:** to get.

flooded (flud´ əd) *v.* Past tense of **flood:** to cover with water.

fluttering (flut´ ər ing´) *v.* Moving or flying with quick flapping movements.

G

giants (jī´ ənts) *n.* Plural of **giant:** an imaginary creature that looks like a huge person and has great strength.

glides (glīdz) *v.* Moves in a smooth way.

glimpse (glimps) *n.* A quick view.

glossy (glo´ sē) *adj.* Bright and shiny.

graduated (graj´ o͞o ā´ təd) *v.* Past tense of **graduate:** to finish school.

grape pickers (grāp pi´ kərz) *n.* Plural of **grape picker:** Someone who picks grapes from vines.

Pronunciation Key: at; lāte; câre; fäther; set; mē; it; kīte; ox; rōse; ô in bought; coin; bŏŏk; tōō; form; out; up; ūse; tûrn; ə sound in about, chicken, pencil, cannon, circus; **ch**air; **hw** in **wh**ich; ri**ng**; **sh**op; **th**in; **t̶h**ere; **zh** in trea**s**ure

gratefully (grāt´ fəl ē´) *adv.* In a way that is full of thanks.

grip (grip) *n.* A firm hold.

gurgling (gûr´ gling) *v.* Making a sound like a bubbling liquid.

gushing (gush´ ing) *v.* Pouring out suddenly.

gymnasium (jim nā´ zē əm) *n.* A room or building with equipment for physical exercise or training and for indoor sports.

hare (hâr) *n.* A kind of rabbit.

hawk (hôk) *n.* A bird with a sharp, hooked beak, strong claws, and sharp eyesight.

herd (hûrd) *n.* A group of animals.

herd

hero (hēr´ ō) *n.* A person who does brave or important things to help others.

honors (on´ ərz) *n.* Plural of **honor:** something given to show respect.

hue (hū) *n.* Color.

imitator (im´i tā´ tûr) *n.* One who copies something or someone.

inform (in fôrm´) *v.* To tell.

introduced (in´ trə dūsd´) *v.* Past tense of **introduce:** to bring into use.

invitations (in və tā´ shənz) *n.* Plural of **invitation:** a written or spoken request to do something.

issued (ish´ ōōd) *v.* Past tense of **issue:** to send out.

katydid (kā´ tē did´) *n.* A large green grasshopper.

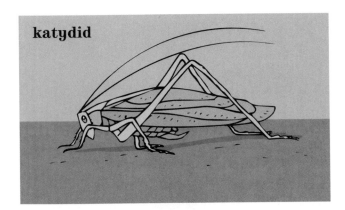

katydid

kingdom (king´ dəm) *n.* A country ruled by a king or queen.

L

laws (lôz) *n.* Plural of **law:** a rule made by a government.

lead (lēd) *n.* The first position.

leak (lēk) *n.* A hole or tear that lets something pass through by accident.

leaping (lēp´ ing) *v.* Jumping.

leather (let͡h´ ər) *n.* Material made from animal skin.

limb (lim) *n.* A branch of a tree.

limb

limping (limp´ ing) *v.* Walking with difficulty.

Pronunciation Key: at; l**ā**te; c**â**re; f**ä**ther; s**e**t; m**ē**; **i**t; k**ī**te; **o**x; r**ō**se; **ô** in b**ou**ght; c**oi**n; b**oo**k; t**oo**; f**o**rm; **ou**t; **u**p; **ū**se; t**û**rn; **ə** sound in **a**bout, chick**e**n, penc**i**l, cann**o**n, circ**u**s; **ch**air; **hw** in **wh**ich; ri**ng**; **sh**op; **th**in; **th**ere; **zh** in trea**s**ure

livestock (līv´ stok) *n.* Farm animals, such as cows, sheep, horses, or pigs.

marshes (marsh´ əz) *n.* Plural of **marsh:** a low, wet land.

match (mach) *v.* To be the same as.

meadow (med´ ō) *n.* A field of grass.

meadow

memory (mem´ ə rē) *n.* A person or thing recalled.

mimicry (mim´ i krē) *n.* The act of copying.

minister (min´ ə stər) *n.* The leader in a church.

mirror (mir´ ər) *n.* A smooth surface that shows the image of the person or thing in front of it by reflecting light.

mountain lion (moun´ tən lī´ ən) *n.* A large wild cat that lives in the mountains.

mural (myûr´ əl) *n.* A picture painted on a wall or ceiling.

mysterious (mis tēr´ ē əs) *adj.* Difficult to understand or explain.

natural (nach´ ər əl) *adj.* Acting on information one is born with.

north (nôrth) *adv.* A direction.

numb (num) *v.* Having no feeling.

O

orchid (ôr´ kid) *n.* A type of flower.

orchid

P

pale (pāl) *adj.* Light in color.

patches (pach´ iz) *n.* Plural of **patch:** a small area.

patterns (pat´ ərnz) *n.* Plural of **pattern:** the order colors, shapes, or lines.

plains (plānz) *n.* An area of flat land.

platter (pla´ tər) *n.* A dish for meat.

platter

pond (pond) *n.* A small lake.

popular (pop´ yə lər) *adj.* Liked or accepted by many people.

pounding (poun´ ding) *v.* Beating.

powerful (pou´ ûr fəl) *adj.* Having great effect on someone or something.

practiced (prak´ tisd) *v.* Past tense of **practice:** to do some action over and over again to gain skill.

prejudice (prej´ ə dis) *n.* Unfair treatment of a group of people.

pretenders (prē tend´ ûrz) *n.* Plural of **pretender:** something that makes believe it is something else.

proceeds (prō´ sēdz) *v.* Moves on or continues.

proclamation (prok´ lə mā´ shən) *n.* A statement to the people.

protective (prə tek´ tiv) *adj.* Keeps out of danger or away from harm.

protests (prō´ tests) *n.* Plural of **protest:** a public demonstration of disapproval or dislike.

puffing (puf´ fing) *v.* Breathing in short breaths.

Q

qualified (kwol´ ə fīd´) *v.* Past tense of **qualify:** to be able to do a job or task.

R

ranch (ranch) *n.* A large farm.

ranch

recognized (rek´ əg nīzd´) *v.* Past tense of **recognize:** to know and remember from before.

recycling (rē sī´ kling) *v.* Using throwaway items for another purpose.

reeds (rēdz) *n.* Plural of **reed:** tall grass.

relative (rel´ ə tiv) *n.* One thing that has a connection to or belongs to the same family as something else.

replied (ri plīd´) *v.* Past tense of **reply:** to answer.

reptiles (rep´ tīlz) *n.* Plural of **reptile:** a cold-blooded animal with a backbone that has dry, scaly skin and moves by crawling on its stomach or creeping on short legs.

reservation (re´ zər vā´ shən) *n.* Land where Native Americans live.

riots (rī´ əts) *n.* Plural of **riot:** a noisy and violent disorder caused by a crowd of people.

rooting (roo´ ting) *v.* Cheering.

rows (rōs) *n.* Plural of **row:** a series of people or things arranged in a line.

rugged (rug´ id) *adj.* Rough and uneven.

rumble (rum´ bəl) *n.* A heavy, deep, rolling sound.

rumbling (rum´ bling) *v.* Making a heavy, deep, rolling sound.

S

scent (sent) *n.* A smell.

screamed (skrēmd) *v.* Past tense of **scream:** to make a loud, shrill cry or sound.

section (sek´ shən) *n.* A part.

sesame (se´ sə mē) *n.* A tropical Asian plant bearing small, flat seeds used as food and as a source of oil.

sesame

Pronunciation Key: at; l**ā**te; c**â**re; f**ä**ther; s**e**t; m**ē**; **i**t; k**ī**te; **o**x; r**ō**se; **ô** in b**o**ught; c**oi**n; b**oo**k; t**oo**; f**o**rm; **ou**t; **u**p; **ū**se; t**û**rn; **ə** sound in **a**bout, chick**e**n, penc**i**l, cann**o**n, circ**u**s; **ch**air; **hw** in **wh**ich; ri**ng**; **sh**op; **th**in; **th**ere; **zh** in trea**s**ure

shadow (shad´ ō) *n.* A dark area or figure made when rays of light are blocked by a person or thing.

shed (shed) *v.* To lose hair.

shed (shed) *n.* A small building used for storing things.

shifted (shif´ təd) *v.* Past tense of **shift:** to change position.

shouted (shout´ ed) *v.* Past tense of **shout:** to yell.

shoved (shuvd) *v.* Past tense of **shove:** to push with force.

shucked (shukd) *v.* Past tense of **shuck:** to take off.

shuffled (shuf´ əld) *v.* Past tense of **shuffle:** to drag one's feet while walking.

slaves (slāvs) *n.* Plural of **slave:** a person who is owned by another person.

sleek (slēk) *adj.* Smooth and shiny.

slender (slen´ dûr) *adj.* Thin.

slipped (slipd) *v.* Past tense of **slip:** to put on.

snapped (snapd) *v.* Past tense of **snap:** to move quickly and sharply.

sneaky (snē´ kē) *adj.* Trying to keep from being seen.

snowdrift (snō´ drift´) *n.* Snow piled up by the wind.

snowdrift

spattering (spa´ tûr ing) *v.* Splashing with small drops.

speckles (spe´ kəlz) *n.* Plural of **speckle:** a small spot.

spied (spīd) *v.* Past tense of **spy:** to notice.

spine (spīn) *n.* The column of bones in the back.

spines (spīnz) *n.* Plural of **spine:** a sharp point on a plant or animal.

spine

sprout (sprout) *v.* To begin to grow.

squinted (skwin´ təd) *v.* Past tense of **squint:** to look with the eyes partially closed.

stalks (stôks) *n.* Plural of **stalk:** the main stem of a plant.

startled (stär´ təld) *v.* Past tense of **startle:** to surprise.

stomping (stom´ ping) *v.* Walking heavily.

strand (strand) *n.* One of the threads in a rope.

stream (strēm) *n.* A small body of flowing water.

strike (strīk) *v.* To stop work in order to get better pay and working conditions.

strolled (strōld) *v.* Past tense of **stroll:** to walk in a slow, relaxed way.

stubby (stub´ ē) *adj.* Short and thick.

445

Pronunciation Key: at; l**ā**te; c**â**re; f**ä**ther; s**e**t; m**ē**; **i**t; k**ī**te; **o**x; r**ō**se; **ô** in b**o**ught; c**oi**n; b**oo**k; t**oo**; f**o**rm; **ou**t; **u**p; **ū**se; t**û**rn; **ə** sound in **a**bout, chick**e**n, penc**i**l, cann**o**n, circ**u**s; **ch**air; **hw** in **wh**ich; ri**ng**; **sh**op; **th**in; **th**ere; **zh** in trea**s**ure

stump (stump) *n*. The part of a tree that is left after the tree has been cut down.

stump

succeed (sək sēd´) *v*. To come after and take the place of.

successor (sək ses´ ûr) *n*. A person who takes over another person's job.

support (sə pôrt´) *v*. To provide for.

surroundings (sə roun´ dingz) *n*. The area around a person or thing.

swarmed (swormd) *v*. Past tense of **swarm:** to move in a large group.

sways (swāz) *v*. Moves back and forth.

swirling (swûr´ ling) *v*. Spinning around.

temper (tem´ pûr) *n*. Mood.

tended (ten´ dəd) *v*. Past tense of **tend:** to take care of someone or something.

tender (ten´ dûr) *adj*. Soft.

throughout (throo out´) *prep*. In every part of.

tin (tin) *n*. A soft silvery metal.

tips (tips) *n.* Plural of **tip:** the end part or point.

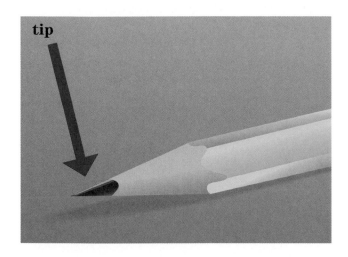

tip

transferred (trans fûrd´) *v.* Past tense of **transfer:** to move something from one place to another.

treated (trēt´ əd) *v.* Past tense of **treat:** to behave toward or deal with in a certain way.

trembling (trem´ bling) *v.* Shaking.

trickling (trik´ ling) *v.* Flowing drop by drop.

trout (trout) *n.* A long bony fish.

trout

twitching (twich´ ing) *v.* Moving with a sudden jerk.

unaware (un´ ə wâr´) *adj.* Not watchful or mindful.

union (ūn´ yən) *n.* A group of workers who join together to get better pay and working conditions.

village (vil´ ij) *n.* A small group of houses.

violence (vī´ ə ləns) *n.* Strong physical force used to harm.

Pronunciation Key: **a**t; l**ā**te; c**â**re; f**ä**ther; s**e**t; m**ē**; **i**t; k**ī**te; **o**x; r**ō**se; **ô** in b**o**ught; c**oi**n; b**oo**k; t**oo**; f**o**rm; **ou**t; **u**p; **ū**se; t**û**rn; **ə** sound in **a**bout, chick**e**n, penc**i**l, cann**o**n, circ**u**s; **ch**air; **hw** in **wh**ich; ri**ng**; **sh**op; **th**in; **th**ere; **zh** in trea**s**ure

volunteer (vol´ ən tîr´) *n.* A person who offers to help, often without pay.

wading (wād´ ing) *v.* Walking through water.

washed away (wôsht´ ə wā´) *v.* Past tense of **wash away:** to destroy by flowing water.

weakened (wē´ kənd) *v.* Past tense of **weaken:** to grow less strong.

whirlwind (hwûrl´ wind´) *n.* Wind that moves in a circle with great force.

windmills (wind´ milz) *n.* Plural of **windmill:** a machine that uses the power of the wind to turn sails.

windmill

wiser (wī´ zûr) *adj.* Smarter.

wits (wits) *n.* Wisdom.

Photo Credits